The Blackbirch Visual Encyclopedia

Planet Earth

BLACKBIRCH®
PRESS

THOMSON

GALE

San Diego • Detroit • New York • San Francisco • Cleveland • New Haven, Conn. • Waterville, Maine • London • Munich

CONTENTS

Text credit: Steve Parker, Nicholas Harris

Consultant credit: Susanna van Rose, writer and geologist
Professor Michael Benton, Department of Geology, Bristol University

Illustration credit: Julian Baker, Alessandro Bartolozzi, Tim Hayward, Gary Hincks, Steve Kirk, Lee Montgomery, Steve Noon, Nicki Palin, Sebastian Quigley, Alessandro Rabatti, Claudia Saraceni, Peter David Scott, Roger Stewart, Thomas Trojer, David Wright

Photograph on page 5: Michael Giannechini/Science Photo Library; on page 58: The Illustrated London News Picture Library

> **LIBRARY OF CONGRESS CATALOGING-IN-PUBLICATION DATA**
>
> Harris, Nicholas, 1956-
> Planet earth / Nicholas Harris.
>   p. cm. — (Blackbirch visual encyclopedia)
>   Includes index.
>   Summary: A visual encyclopedia of the history of Earth, including facts about the land, plants, and animals.
>   ISBN 1-56711-514-4 (lib. bdg. : alk. paper)
>   1. Earth—Juvenile literature. [1. Earth—Encyclopedias.] I. Series.
> QB631.4 .P532 2003
> 550—dc21   2002018664

Printed in Singapore
10 9 8 7 6 5 4 3 2 1

CONTENTS

PLANET EARTH

OUR PLANET EARTH is the fifth largest of the nine planets which go around, or orbit, our nearest star—the Sun. Earth speeds through space at about 19 miles (30 km) every second, taking one year to complete one orbit. In addition the planet spins round like a top once every 24 hours. This makes the Sun appear to rise at dawn, pass across the sky, and set at dusk, giving us day and night. Earth is not quite a perfect ball or sphere shape. It is 7,926 miles (12,756 km) across its equator (middle) and 7,900 miles (12,714 km) from pole to pole (top to bottom). The distance around the equator is 24,901.5 miles (40,075 km), and 24,860 miles (40,008 km) from one pole around to the other and back again.

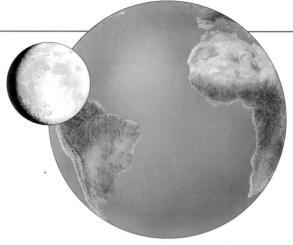

Earth's closest neighbor in space is the Moon. It is 2,159 miles (3,475 km) across, about a quarter the width of Earth. Its volume is around one-thirtieth that of Earth. The rocks that make up the Moon are not as heavy or dense as Earth rocks, so the Moon weighs only one-eightieth as much as Earth.

Earth is the "third rock from the Sun." It is the third planet out from our nearest star, and made mainly of rocky material.

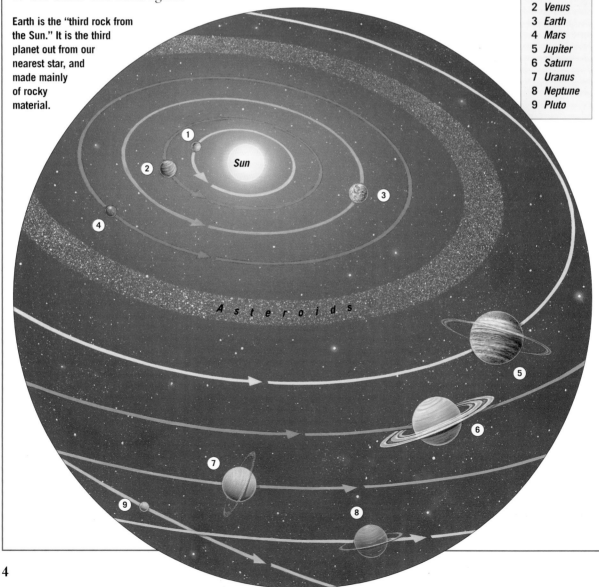

Asteroids

Sun

KEY
1 Mercury
2 Venus
3 Earth
4 Mars
5 Jupiter
6 Saturn
7 Uranus
8 Neptune
9 Pluto

MAGNETIC EARTH

EARTH has its own magnetism—an invisible field of magnetic force all around us. Too weak to notice in daily life, the magnetic field affects iron-based materials and other magnets. We can detect it using a magnetic compass. The compass needle is a long, thin magnet that lines itself up with Earth's magnetism to point north-south. This helps us to read maps and find our way in remote places.

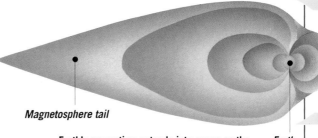

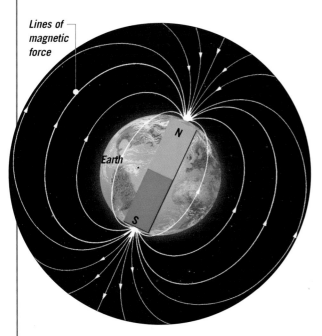

Lines of magnetic force

Earth

Earth's magnetic field is strongest at two places, the North and South Magnetic Poles, where it is directed straight down into the ground. It is as though there was a giant bar magnet inside the planet.

Magnetosphere tail

Earth

Earth's magnetism extends into space as the magnetosphere. High-energy particles from the Sun, the solar wind, "blow" against one side and make it teardrop shaped.

Solar particles

The magnetic field stretches into space and protects us from the Sun's high-energy particles. Some are attracted by the magnetic poles, however, and produce giant curtains of glowing light in the night sky, known as aurorae (above).

Earth's magnetic field is probably created by forces produced in the outer core, a layer of iron that lies some 1,802 miles (2,900 km) below the surface *(see page 6)*. Because of extreme pressure at this depth, it is incredibly hot—more than 7,232°F (4,000°C). At this temperature, the iron is liquid. Heat currents cause the liquid metal to swirl around. The currents are themselves twisted by the spinning motion of Earth into corkscrewlike patterns, called "rollers." These giant movements make electricity which, in turn, creates a magnetic field.

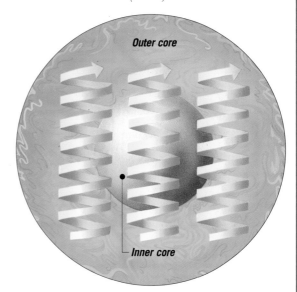

Outer core

Inner core

Scientists believe that massive amounts of flowing heat energy inside Earth, combined with the planet's daily spinning motion, make the semiliquid rocks flow in spiral patterns. These generate electricity, producing a magnetic field.

INSIDE EARTH

ON THE OUTSIDE, Earth seems hard and solid. But if you could drill a deep hole almost 3,977 miles (6,400 km) down to the center of the planet, you would notice many changes as you descend. It becomes warm, then hot. The average increase in temperature is about 37.4°F (3°C) for every 328 feet (100 m) of depth. Soon it is so hot that the rocks are not solid but melted or molten. You pass through layers of rocky material, from the hard crust on the outside, through the thick mantle, to the liquid outer core. When you reach the inner core at the center there is no rock. The core is made of almost solid metal.

THE CRUST

No one has bored a hole nearly this deep. The farthest we have drilled down is about 9 miles (15 km), which is part way through the crust. The crust is thinner in proportion to the whole Earth than the skin on an apple. The crust itself is solid rock and varies in depth. Under the oceans it is about 3–6 miles (5–10 km) thick (with the ocean above) and made mainly of basalt-type rocks. Under the main landmasses, or continents, it is 22–43.5 miles (35–70 km) thick and chiefly granite-type rocks. The taller the mountains above, the deeper the crust below. The crust is not one solid ball-shaped shell. It is cracked into large slowly moving plates (see page 8).

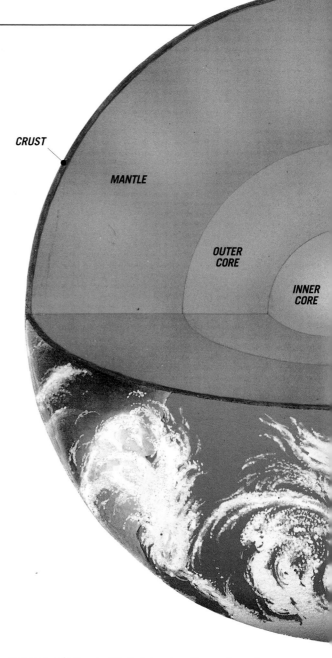

CRUST

MANTLE

OUTER CORE

INNER CORE

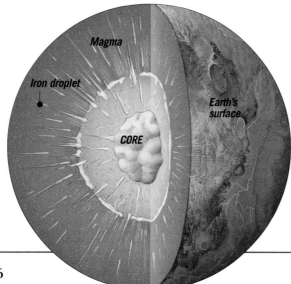

Magma

Iron droplet

Earth's surface

CORE

The four main layers of Earth (above) are the crust, mantle, outer core, and inner core. At the base of the crust is a boundary called the Moho (Mohorovicic discontinuity). This separates the crust from the mantle and the temperature here is about 2,732°F (1,500°C). The mantle is about 1,802 miles (2,900 km) thick. The next layer is the outer core which is 1,367 miles (2,200 km) thick. At the center is the inner core, a solid ball of iron with a radius of about 1,553 miles (2,500 km).

Some 4.6 billion years ago Earth (along with the Sun and other planets) formed from clouds of gas and dust in space. Some of this matter clumped together to form the early Earth, which warmed up and glowed red hot (see page 34). Iron was the heaviest substance so it began to sink through the molten magma as droplets. These collected into drops, then larger blobs. Gradually they clumped at the center of the young planet to form the inner core (left).

THE CORE

At the base of the mantle, there is a sudden change. The material is no longer rock, but metal—mainly iron plus small amounts of nickel. In the outer core, the temperature rises with depth to more than 5,432°F (3,000°C) near the boundary with the inner core. The iron of the outer core is liquid, and flows in giant corkscrewlike currents or "rollers." These probably produce the magnetic field of Earth *(see page 5)*. The temperature rises still more at the inner core, to perhaps up to 13,530°F (7,500°C) at the center of the planet. But the enormous pressure—several million times that at the surface—means that the iron crystals are squashed into a solid ball.

How do we know about Earth's interior, if no one has ever drilled deep into Earth? Evidence comes from the way that shock waves from earthquakes pass around and through Earth *(see page 13),* and from studying meteorites. Some earthquake shock waves do not travel through the outer core, telling us that this part is liquid. We know the core must be made of iron because we can compare it with the composition of iron meteorites, thought to be the remnants of the core of an ancient, Earth-like planet which broke up long ago.

Heat flows within Earth, and slowly from the center to the outside, by the movements of the molten and "plastic" rocks in the mantle. These flow in giant circles, called convection currents. Their motion causes continental drift and seafloor spreading *(see page 8).*

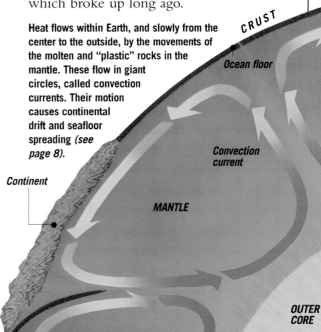

CRUST

Ocean floor

Convection current

Continent

MANTLE

OUTER CORE

THE MANTLE

The mantle also has two layers. Its outer part is about 373 miles (600 km) thick and made of crystals of rock with molten or liquid rock between them. Its temperature is about 3,632°F (2,000°C) and the molten rock, known as magma, can flow like hot tarmac. It is under great pressure and sometimes bursts out of holes or cracks at weak points in the surface of the crust, as the red-hot lava of volcanic eruptions. The pressure in the inner mantle is so great that the rock here is solid—but not completely rigid. It is "plastic" and, very gradually, moves.

RESTLESS EARTH

THE ATLANTIC OCEAN gets wider by about the width of your thumb every year, pushing North and South America away from Europe and Africa. The Himalayan Mountains, already the highest in the world, grow taller by about the length of your thumb every year. Many other parts of Earth are moving and changing shape, too. This is because Earth's outer layer is divided into enormous curved pieces called lithospheric plates, which fit together like a ball-shaped jigsaw. There are six large plates and about 12 to 15 smaller ones, and they are continually on the move. The theory of plate tectonics explains how this happens.

Each plate consists of a piece of Earth's outer layer, the crust, plus a portion below it of a thin layer of outer mantle. Together the crust and thin slice of outer mantle make up the layer known as the lithosphere. Its depth varies from 43.5–50 miles (70–80 km) below the oceans to 62–93 miles (100–150 km) where there are continents. Under the lithosphere is a slightly deeper part of the mantle about 62 miles (100 km) thick, called the aesthenosphere. This is partly molten and allows the plates to slide about over it. In fact the slow flowing of the mantle, due to the enormous heat and pressure within, pushes the plates and makes them slide around the surface of the planet. As they do so, they carry the continental landmasses like giant rafts.

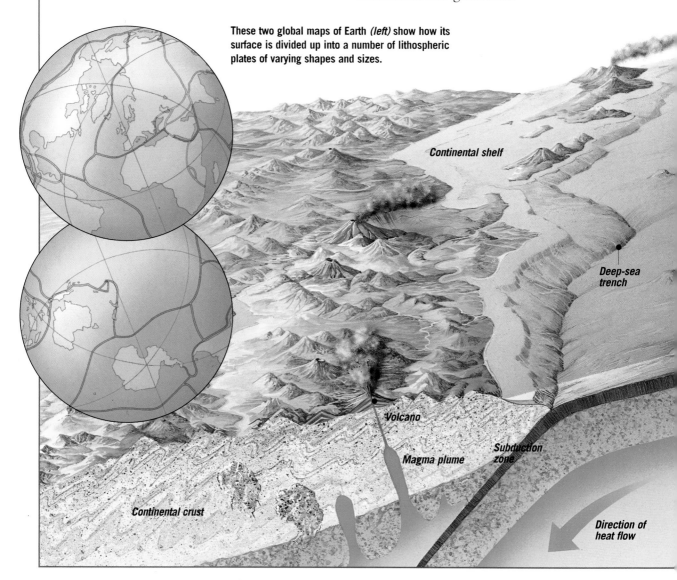

These two global maps of Earth *(left)* show how its surface is divided up into a number of lithospheric plates of varying shapes and sizes.

Continental shelf

Deep-sea trench

Volcano

Magma plume

Subduction zone

Continental crust

Direction of heat flow

SEAFLOOR SPREADING

The lithospheric plates fit together tightly. As they move, they rub and grind their edges against each other. In some places the edges crash into each other and crumple, pushing up mountains. In other places, hot liquid rock wells up from deep below, into the crack or boundary between the oceanic crusts of two plates. The molten rock cools and solidifies, adding to the edges of the two plates as they move apart. This process is called seafloor spreading and it makes the whole ocean wider. The crack between the ocean plates is called the mid-oceanic ridge.

Convergent boundary (collision zone)

Mid-oceanic ridge

Transform fault

Plates meet at three types of boundaries. At a mid-oceanic ridge, new crust is made as the plates push apart. At a convergent boundary, oceanic crust is lost as a thinner oceanic plate is forced down under a thicker continental one (subduction), or is crumpled up into mountains when continental plates collide. At a transform fault, the plates slide past each other.

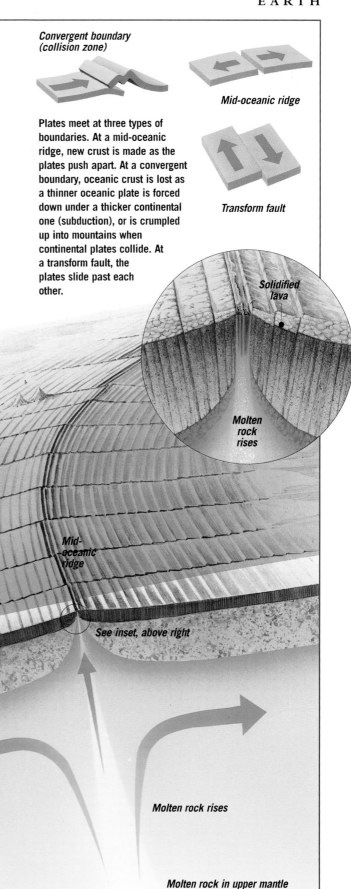

Solidified lava

Molten rock rises

Abyssal plain

Seamount

Mid-oceanic ridge

Ocean surface

See inset, above right

Oceanic crust

When an oceanic plate collides with a continental plate, the edge of the thinner, denser ocean plate slides beneath it in a subduction zone. The rocks of the ocean floor sink deeper and deeper into Earth and melt. Some of this molten rock rises through the continental crust, erupting at the surface as volcanoes.

Convection currents in upper mantle (see page 7)

Molten rock rises

Molten rock in upper mantle

OCEAN FLOOR

ABOUT 71 percent of our planet is covered with water. The largest ocean is the Pacific, which covers 64 million square miles (166 million km²)—almost the same area as all other seas and oceans added together. The landscape around us has tall mountains, wide plains, winding valleys, and deep ravines. Under the waves the seascape has the same features but on an even bigger scale. The highest mountain above sea level is Everest in the Himalayas, at 29,028 feet (8,848 m), but the tallest mountain from base to peak is Mauna Kea on the Pacific island of Hawaii, at 33,480 feet (10,205 m) —with 19,685 feet (6,000 m) below the waves. Everest would disappear into the deepest part of the ocean, the narrow Marianas Trench in the north-west Pacific near Japan, at 35,797 feet (10,911 m) deep. The average depth of the Pacific is 12,959 feet (3,950 m). Its wide abyssal plains cover almost as much area as all Earth's land.

The true edge of a continent is not its coastline. From here the sea bed extends about 31–62 miles (50–100 km), yet the water is less than 656 feet (200 m) deep. This ledge, the continental shelf, is part of the continent. At its edge, it plunges steeply about 6,561–8,202 feet (2,000–2,500 m) down the continental slope, then further down the less steep continental rise, to the main ocean floor. This is the abyssal plain, lying at 13,123 –14,763 feet (4,000–4,500 m) deep.

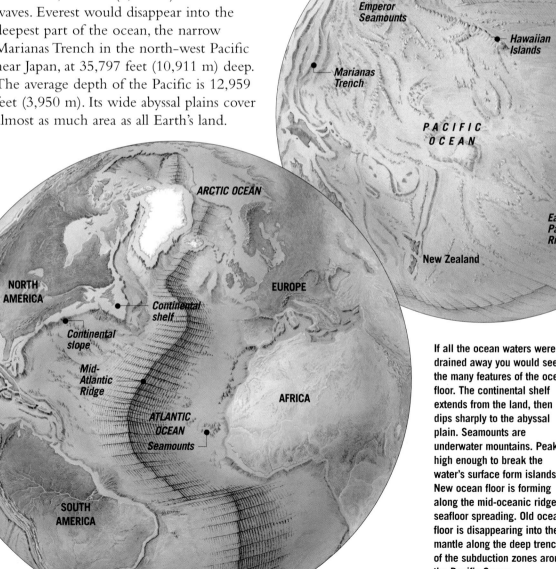

ASIA
Aleutian Trench
NORTH AMERICA
Emperor Seamounts
Hawaiian Islands
Marianas Trench
PACIFIC OCEAN
East Pacific Rise
New Zealand

ARCTIC OCEAN
NORTH AMERICA
EUROPE
Continental shelf
Continental slope
Mid-Atlantic Ridge
AFRICA
ATLANTIC OCEAN
Seamounts
SOUTH AMERICA

If all the ocean waters were drained away you would see the many features of the ocean floor. The continental shelf extends from the land, then dips sharply to the abyssal plain. Seamounts are underwater mountains. Peaks high enough to break the water's surface form islands. New ocean floor is forming along the mid-oceanic ridge by seafloor spreading. Old ocean floor is disappearing into the mantle along the deep trenches of the subduction zones around the Pacific Ocean.

FOLDS AND FAULTS

SLIDING plates and drifting continents *(see page 8)* are responsible for some of Earth's major landscape features. As a large slab or plate of Earth's surface is squeezed, the solid rock slowly wrinkles and crumples. Its layers become wavy folds. The land's surface is pushed up as a series of hills or even mountains. The wind, rain, sun, ice, snow and other forces of nature *(see page 18)* may wear down the folds as fast as they push up, keeping the surface low and rounded. But if the folds rise more quickly they form high, jagged peaks. The world's great mountains, including the Himalayas in Asia, Andes in South America, Rockies in North America, and Alps in Europe, are all fold mountains.

In other places, rocks are stretched or bent and they crack or split along weak points. These cracks are known as faults. They may be straight or zigzag and form narrow slits or wide valleys. A block or strip of land sometimes slips down between two cracks to make a valley with steep slopes on either side, called a rift valley. Rifting can also make mountains, as the rocks on either side move in and squeeze the central block upward. Raised blocks are called horsts and those which slip down are grabens.

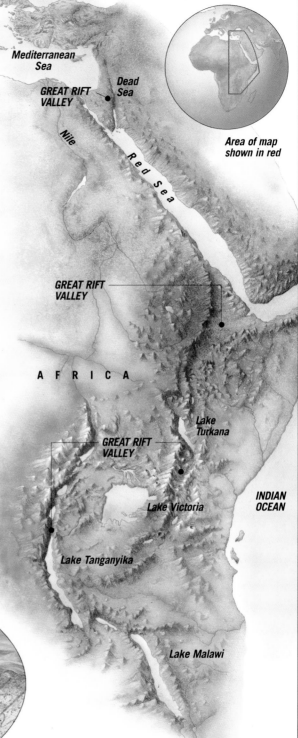

Area of map shown in red

The biggest gash in Earth's land is the Great Rift Valley. This series of rifts runs from the eastern Mediterranean south-east through the Dead Sea and Red Sea, then south across East Africa through Lake Turkana. It divides around Lake Victoria to continue south to Lakes Tanganyika and Malawi. The valley system is some 3,106 miles (5,000 km) long and widens by up to .79 inches (2 cm) in places each year. In millions of years the Red Sea may become a broad ocean and seawater may flood into the valley *(see page 59)*.

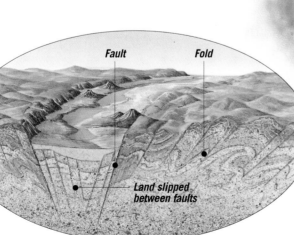

Fault   Fold

Land slipped between faults

A cutaway view reveals how the landscape is shaped by massive forces that crumple and crack solid rock. A wide slab has slipped down between several cracks or faults to form a rift valley with a wide floor and steep sides. To either side of the rift valley the rocks are bent into folds, with some almost tipped right over.

EARTHQUAKES

THERE ARE about 6,000 noticeable earthquakes each year. Scientific devices called seismometers on continuous "quake watch" detect them all. Nine out of ten of these earthquakes are too small or occur in very remote regions so they are only of interest to scientists. Another 30 to 40 cause small-scale problems, while 10 to 20 cause major damage and make headlines. Every 5 to 10 years a massive quake results in great loss of life and devastates a wide area.

An earthquake happens when the plates which form Earth's outer layer *(see page 8)* suddenly slip past each, snap or make some other rapid movement, especially along their edges or at cracks (faults).

The sudden jolt of a quake usually lasts not more than a few minutes and may be over in just a few seconds. It spreads out from a place called the focus. A shallow focus is down to 43 miles (70 km) below the surface, an intermediate one 43–186 miles (70–300 km), and deep focus below 186 miles (300 km) Juddering shock or seismic waves spread out in all directions through the rocks. They reach the surface first at the epicenter, directly above the focus, and are usually strongest here.

Many earthquakes occur along subduction zones where one lithospheric plate with oceanic crust grinds down below the edge of a continent. The main slippage is deep underground at a point called the focus.

Ocean floor

Trench

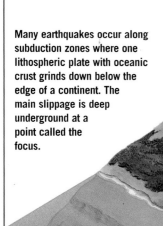

PACIFIC OCEAN

Location of major earthquakes (shown by red dots).

Movement of continental crust

Focus

Seismic wave

Movement of ocean crust

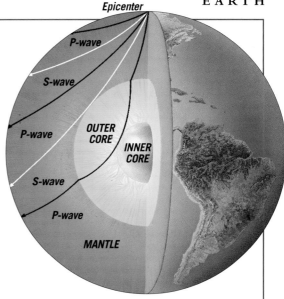

Cities around the Pacific Rim suffer regular quakes. Tokyo was devastated in 1923.

The shock waves reach Earth's surface around the epicenter, spreading out like ripples on a pond. The immensely powerful vibrations of a massive earthquake travel around and through the whole planet, making it tremble and shake for up to 20 minutes. Most earthquakes happen along the edges of Earth's huge plates, especially where these are actively moving (often resulting in volcanoes, too). High-risk regions are the "Pacific Rim," around the shores of the Pacific Ocean, Southeast Asia (Philippines and Indonesia), from northern India west to southern Europe. Some large earthquakes also happen away from the plate edges.

There are several types of shock waves. P (primary) waves travel quickly through Earth, although its inner layers bend them. S (secondary) waves are slower and cannot go through the liquid outer core.

Two scales measure earthquakes. The Mercalli scale shows how much damage is caused, from 1 (not felt) to 12 (total devastation), while the Richter scale measures the magnitude of the shock.

Earthquakes under the sea set off underwater ripples. These reach land and rear up to form huge waves, called tsunamis.

VOLCANOES

WHEN A VOLCANO erupts and hurls out its red-hot rock, this is one of the most awesome events of nature. It happens at a hole, crack, or weak point in the solid rocks of Earth's crust. Melted rock called magma from deep below forces its way up under incredible temperature and pressure. As it emerges it is called lava. When it cools and hardens, it forms a type of rock known as igneous rock *(see page 16)*.

Some lava is thin and runny. It oozes like boiling syrup from the volcano and spreads over a wide area. As it cools, it turns into a "shield" of solid rock known as basalt. Each time the volcano erupts it adds to the shield, in layers of lava up to 33 feet (10 m) thick. Known as shield volcanoes, the eruptions are gentle.

In explosive eruptions, lava is thick and sticky. It moves slowly and hardens near the volcano's vent or crater. As this type of volcano erupts time after time, the lava builds up to form a tall, steep-sided mountain known as a cone.

The temperature of lava erupting from a volcano can be more than 1,832°F (1,000°C). It may take months to harden. Volcanoes eject other substances, too: gases and fumes rich in sulphur. Some give out clouds of ash or cinders that fly high in the air. The cinders may fall near the volcano and build up a cinder cone. Some volcanoes have such explosive power that they blast out huge lumps of molten rock as big as houses. These volcanic bombs crash to the ground nearby. The ash is often blown away by the wind and may fall over a very wide area.

This 5-stage sequence shows the eruption of Santorini's volcano in the Mediterranean Sea in about 1450 B.C.

Lava, ash and gases

Crater

Side vent

Main vent

Hardened layers of lava and ash from previous eruptions

Crust

Magma

An active volcano regularly erupts lava, ash, fumes, and other materials. In very active volcanoes, this happens almost continuously. In others, there are weeks or months between eruptions. When a volcano has not erupted for many years or centuries, but still might in the future, it is dormant. When there have been no eruptions for tens of thousands of years the volcano is described as extinct. Some volcanoes blast out gas and spurt red-hot lava in a spectacular eruption. Others erupt more explosively, producing clouds of ash and gas. On land, most magma oozes slowly to the surface over very long time periods without explosive power. It emerges from long cracks or fissures and spreads out to form low mounds of volcanic rock.

WHERE VOLCANOES ERUPT

Most volcanoes are situated along the edges of the giant, jigsawlike lithospheric plates which make up Earth's surface *(see page 8)*. The boundaries between plates have many weak points. In particular, volcanoes form along subduction zones where one plate slides down beneath another. As the lower plate melts back into the mantle its gases and lighter molten rock "boil" and force their way up through cracks with enormous pressure, causing eruptions.

Rainwater may trickle down through cracks in rocks to deeper layers where it is heated by magma. It comes blasting back out as a fountain of steam, spray, and hot water known as a geyser.

All along the mid-oceanic ridge *(right)*, molten rock seeps into the ocean floor from the mantle below in a series of continually erupting volcanoes. Hot, mineral-rich water and gas bubble from deep-sea hydrothermal vents that lie near these fissure volcanoes.

The typical cone-shaped volcanoes on land may seem huge and powerful. But they make up less than one-hundredth of all the volcanic activity on Earth. Most magma oozes to the surface deep underwater, along the cracklike fissures of mid-oceanic ridges *(see page 8)* or through smaller weak "holes" known as hot spots. If underwater volcanoes build cones tall enough they emerge at the surface as islands, such as the Hawaiian Islands in the Pacific and the Canary Islands in the Atlantic.

GREAT VOLCANIC ERUPTIONS

• 1450 B.C. Santorini, Greece
Biggest explosion in ancient times
• A.D. 79 Vesuvius, Italy
Described by Pliny the Younger. Pliny the Elder was killed in the eruption
• 1815 Tambora, Indonesia
Killed 90,000-plus people
• 1883 Krakatau, Java *Heard 3,107 miles (5,000 km) away*
• 1980 Mt. St Helens, US
Filmed as it happened
• 1991 Pinatubo, Philippines
Affected the world's weather for two years

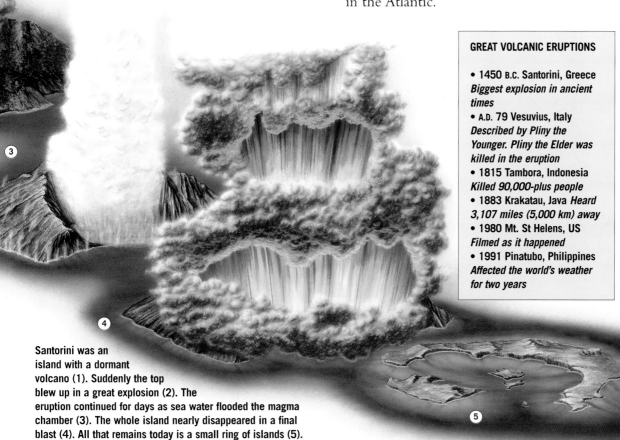

Santorini was an island with a dormant volcano (1). Suddenly the top blew up in a great explosion (2). The eruption continued for days as sea water flooded the magma chamber (3). The whole island nearly disappeared in a final blast (4). All that remains today is a small ring of islands (5).

ROCKS

ROCK is the hard material that makes up Earth's crust. Various combinations of minerals make up hundreds of different types of rocks. For example, the rock sandstone consists mainly of grains of sand pressed and cemented together. Sand is made mainly of the mineral quartz which consists of the chemical elements silicon and oxygen.

All rocks can be divided into three main groups depending on how they formed. Igneous rocks, such as granite and basalt, are formed when magma, molten rock from beneath the Earth's crust, rises, cools, and solidifies. Sedimentary rocks, such as sandstone and mudstone, are made from sand, gravel, mud, and other fragments of rock that result from erosion *(see page 18)*. These settle in layers in lakes, rivers, and seas. As more layers settle on top of each other, the particles are compressed and cemented into sedimentary rock. The third

Most magma rises slowly through the crust and turns into solid rock underground. There, like jelly in a mould, it takes on the shape of its surroundings, resulting in ledges, columns, domes and other shapes.

group, metamorphic rocks, such as marble and slate, are formed when rocks are subjected to such great pressure and heat that their mineral composition is altered.

Rocks are constantly being changed. Weathering attacks all kinds of surface rocks. The eroded fragments form new sedimentary rocks which may sink into Earth, melt, then later cool to become igneous rocks. Alternatively, they may be cooked and crushed deep in the crust, forming metamorphic rocks. This change from one type to another is called the rock cycle *(below)*.

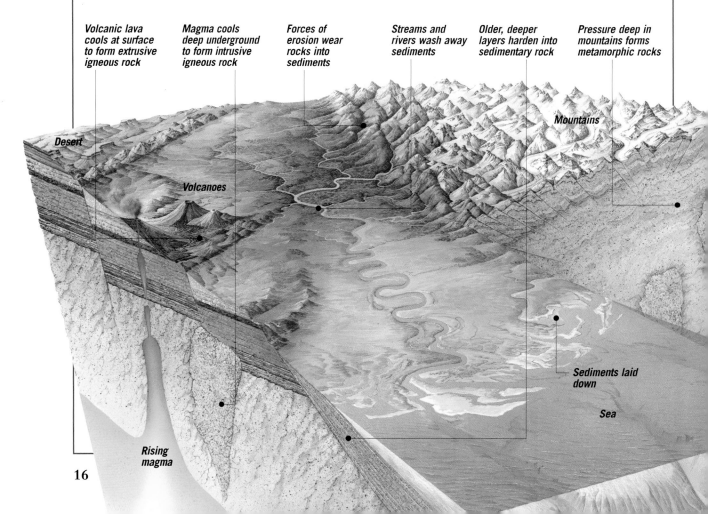

Volcanic lava cools at surface to form extrusive igneous rock

Magma cools deep underground to form intrusive igneous rock

Forces of erosion wear rocks into sediments

Streams and rivers wash away sediments

Older, deeper layers harden into sedimentary rock

Pressure deep in mountains forms metamorphic rocks

Mountains

Desert

Volcanoes

Sediments laid down

Sea

Rising magma

FOSSILS

FOSSILS ARE remains of once-living things preserved in rock. Most living things are eaten or die and their soft parts rot away leaving no trace. But sometimes hard body parts remain, like the shells, bones, teeth, horns, and claws of animals and the bark, cones, and seeds of plants. These are the parts most likely to form fossils. Trace fossils are not actual body parts but signs and traces of living things such as egg shells, footprints, and droppings.

Fossils form in sedimentary rocks. They are destroyed if the rock is heated or squashed too much so they do not occur in igneous or metamorphic rocks. Some sediments contain layer upon layer of fossils, like this shelly limestone. It formed after thousands of ammonites died and their shells piled up on the sea bed.

The hard parts like bones and teeth are buried under sediment particles such as sand grains on a beach, silt on a river bank or mud on a sea bed. Slowly the surrounding water dissolves away the remains and replaces them with rock minerals from the water. Meanwhile the particles around them are also turning into rock. If undisturbed, the remains keep their original shape but they are now solid rock—fossils.

The sticky sap or resin that oozes from trees and other plants may fossilize as a hard yellow substance, amber. This sometimes contains insects and other small animals that were trapped in it, preserved in amazing detail.

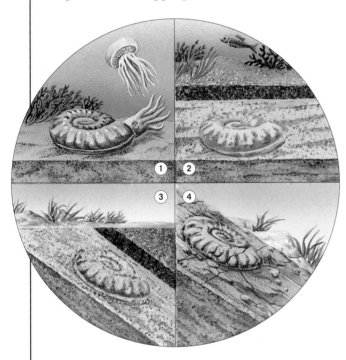

An ammonite, a prehistoric cousin of the octopus and squid, lived in a coiled shell and floated or swam in the sea. When it died its soft, fleshy parts soon rotted away or were eaten (1). Sandy sediments slowly covered the hard shell on the sea bed (2). Both shell and sand gradually turned into rock which was lifted and tilted by massive earth movements (3). Erosion uncovered the fossil shell at the surface (4).

Fossils take many thousands or millions of years to form and are found only in sedimentary rocks *(see opposite)*. Then, as part of great earth movements and the wearing-away forces of erosion, the sediments and their fossils may be exposed at or near the surface. Experts called paleontologists search for fossils, dig them from the ground, study their shapes and structures, and compare them with similar body parts of living things today. This shows the kinds of dinosaurs, mammoths, and other animals and plants that lived millions of years ago.

This is the fossil skeleton of an ichthyosaur *(right)*, a marine reptile from the Age of Dinosaurs *(see page 48)*. A trace fossil of a dinosaur footprint is shown *(below right)*.

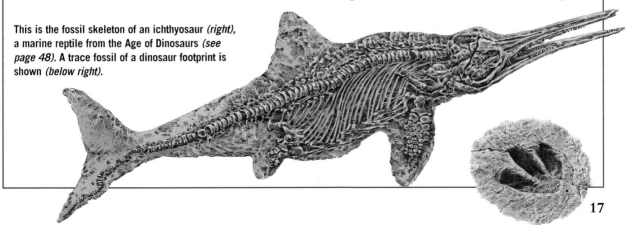

EROSION

OVER THE MILLIONS of years of geological time *(see page 32),* mountain ranges have formed—then disappeared. Continental drift, faulting, and other earth movements have created these mountains. What has happened to them? Most have been worn down by the slow processes of weathering and erosion.

Changes in temperature, rain, and frost all break down the rocks in a process called weathering. Rocks heat up and expand in the hot sun, then cool and contract at night. The temperature changes crack the rock surface and small pieces flake off. Rainwater seeps into crevices in rocks and, as it freezes, it expands with great force and splits off pieces. This is known as frost wedging.

Erosion is the removal of fragments of rock by the action of running water, glaciers, or wind. Rivers, especially if they are fast-flowing or in flood, can carry away pieces of rock. Waves crashing onto cliffs, sometimes hurling pebbles or boulders at the rock, are also powerful forces of erosion.

Weathering wears away higher areas of land fastest *(above).* Ice, wind, and water carry the rocky fragments and deposit them in lower regions such as plains, rivers, and lakes, where they are known as sediments.

The world's most spectacular example of erosion is the Grand Canyon in Arizona, US *(below).* The soft rock layers wore away more easily than the hard layers, which today stand out as near-vertical cliff faces.

THE GRAND CANYON

The Grand Canyon is a great gorge that twists across the dry, rocky region of Arizona, US, for 217 miles (350 km). It formed over the past six million years as earth movements pushed up the land by more than 3,937 feet (1,200 m). The fast-flowing Colorado River has steadily cut into the land to maintain its downward flow to the sea. The result is a steep-sided canyon, on average 10 miles (16 km) wide and 5,249 feet (1,600 m) deep in places. The region's desert climate *(see page 23)* means the softer, upper rock layers have not been washed away.

The river is especially powerful in spring when melting snows in the distant Rockies send floodwaters down the canyon. They sweep along boulders that chip away at the river's bed and banks. As the river cuts deeper, it reveals ancient layers of rock and the fossils they contain. The lowest layers of rocks are 1.7 billion years old. They were themselves once mountains towering thousands of feet above sea level.

The Colorado River once flowed across desert (*above*, 1), but as the land rose (2) it cut a deeper and deeper valley (3).

RIVERS

RIVERS ARE natural channels that carry rain, melted ice, and snow downhill from mountains and uplands to lowlands, lakes, and seas. They support much wildlife in their waters and along their banks. The world's longest rivers are the Nile in Africa and the Amazon in South America, both about 4,101 miles (6,600 km) long. But the Amazon is so wide and fast-flowing, it carries more water than the Nile plus the next five longest rivers combined together. The Amazon gathers water from 2.7 million square miles (7 million km²) of land, an area larger than western Europe.

Glacier

Waterfall

Gorge

A waterfall forms where a river cascades down a cliff, or where its bed changes from hard to softer rock. The river wears down the softer rock more quickly so a "lip" of hard rock forms above it. The world's highest waterfalls are Salto Angel (Angel Falls, *right*) on the Carraro River in Venezuela, South America. The total height is (979 m) with the tallest single drop at (807 m). The water becomes a mist before reaching the bottom.

This river *(right)* begins high in the mountains as the snout of a melting glacier. After receiving a tributary it flows over a waterfall and through a gorge, then forms a network of smaller channels, called braids. On the lowland plains it follows looplike meanders sometimes edged by raised banks of sediment, known as levees. At its mouth it divides into many channels. These trickle through a muddy delta.

Rivers have had great effects on our history. Early towns and cities grew up along them because they provided transportation routes by boat, food such as fish, and water supplies for drinking, cooking, and raising farm crops and animals.

Rivers shape the land as they flow over rocks of varying hardness, widening and deepening their valleys by erosion. The faster they flow the greater their erosive power, and the larger the rocks and amount of sediment they can transport.

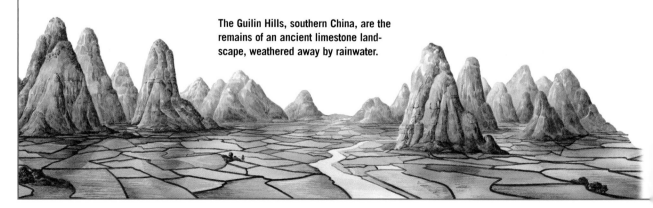

The Guilin Hills, southern China, are the remains of an ancient limestone land-scape, weathered away by rainwater.

A typical river starts as a spring gushing out of the ground, as a melting glacier or as rainwater collecting in small brooks and streams. The river's upper waters usually flow fast and steep. The swift current washes away soil or mud so the bed is stony and the banks are bare. Gradually the slope eases and the river flows more slowly in its middle reaches, widening as smaller rivers, called tributaries, add to it. A slower current results in the river shedding its load of sediment on its bed or its banks, sometimes producing braids. As the river's course becomes flatter it flows in huge curves called meanders across plains, but still follows a downward route. Finally it enters the sea at the river mouth or estuary. The tiny fragments of rock and soil it carries settle as sand and mud banks. It may divide into many channels, forming a delta.

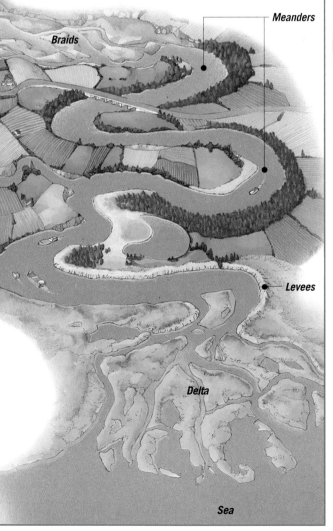

Braids

Meanders

Levees

Delta

Sea

CAVES

CAVES are underground holes in the rock. Some caves open up when the ground splits, as in an earthquake. Some are eroded by waves hurling stones and pebbles at a cliff. But most are made in limestone rocks by a chemical process. Rainwater naturally contains tiny amounts of acid. It trickles into cracks and reacts with the rock's lime substances to dissolve them away. Over thousands of years small cracks are widened into huge caves.

Inside this cave, a stalactite above has merged with a stalagmite below to form a column or pillar of rock. Stalactites and stalagmites can reach 98 feet (30 m) in length.

In a limestone landscape, a stream disappears into a swallow hole, or when the stream no longer flows, a dry pot hole. Underground is a cave system of many chambers, some with underground lakes, and linked by upright shafts and horizontal galleries. As water drips from the ceiling, dissolved minerals in it gradually harden to form icicle-like shapes of rock called stalactites hanging down. Stalagmites grow up from the floor where water containing dissolved minerals drips from the ceiling.

GLACIERS

A GLACIER is a moving mass of ice. Some glaciers snake down mountain valleys, while others such as the ice sheets of Greenland or Antarctica are so huge and thick they almost totally cover the land. Although it is solid, ice can flow down slopes and around bends—although much more slowly than a river, often less than three feet per day. Glaciers occur in very cold regions, high in mountains and in the far north and south polar regions. Ice covers about 5.8 square miles (15 million km²), nearly one-tenth of Earth's land surface. The largest glacier in the world is Antarctica's Lambert Glacier which is usually more than 310 miles (500 km) long.

A glacier is fed by snow. Over many years, the snow piles up at the head of a high valley and compacts into ice. It collects in a cirque, a bowl-shaped feature. Being thick and heavy, the ice moves under the pressure of its own weight, flowing downhill as a glacier. The ice carries pieces of rock loosened by frost weathering and scrapes against the valley sides. It carries this loose rock along in long bands called lateral moraines, or underneath the glacier as subglacial moraine. As two glaciers merge their lateral moraines combine into a medial moraine. Where the ice runs over a steeper slope, it develops cracks known as crevasses. Lower down, the glacier melts at its snout, leaving a pile of the rocks it has carried as a terminal moraine, and a meltwater stream.

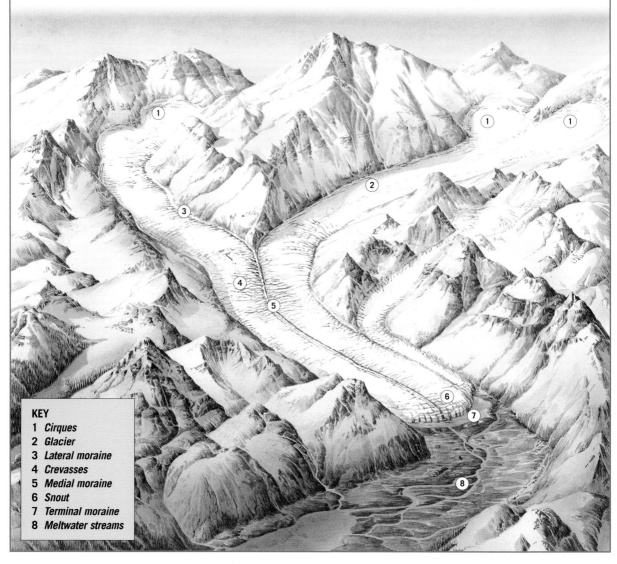

KEY
1 *Cirques*
2 *Glacier*
3 *Lateral moraine*
4 *Crevasses*
5 *Medial moraine*
6 *Snout*
7 *Terminal moraine*
8 *Meltwater streams*

DESERTS

A DESERT is an area with very low rainfall, usually with less than 10 inches (25 cm) of rain (or snow) yearly. It may be hot all year round, as in the Sahara of Africa, or always cold as in Greenland or Antarctica. The Gobi Desert of Central Asia is hot in summer and cold in winter. "Hot" deserts may be bitterly cold at night. The Takla Makan Desert, China, may be a scorching 104°F (40°C) by day yet plunge to −40°F (−40°C) at night.

The Mojave Desert in North America, and the Patagonian Desert of South America have formed because moist winds have dropped their water as rain or snow over nearby mountains. The lands beyond lie in what are known as rain shadows. Deserts like the Gobi form in the middle of huge landmasses far from the main source of moisture, the sea. Most deserts, including the Atacama, Sahara, Kalahari, and Namib deserts, lie in a band to the north and south of the equator. These are the result of global patterns of winds and rainfall.

Wind blows sand into crescent dunes, or barchans, with "horns" pointing downwind. They slowly crawl along with the wind.

Deserts and arid regions cover one-eighth of the world's land area. The driest desert is the Atacama in Chile, South America, with an average of less than 1 millimeter of rain yearly. In some places it has not rained for centuries. The largest desert is the Sahara in Africa, over 3,107 miles (5,000 km) wide and covering 3.4 million square miles (9 million km²). The continent with the largest proportion of desert—about one half its area—is Australia.

Most people think of deserts as vast sandy regions, but only about 20 percent of the world's deserts are sandy. The rest are bare rock, or covered with gravel. The erosive power of the wind and rainstorms sculpts the desert landscape. Storms hurls sand at rocks, producing shapes like arches *(above)* or mushrooms and other strange landscapes.

The Olgas, Australia *(left),* are the result of "onion-skin" weathering. Daily heating and cooling flake rock layers away. Hard rock has resisted erosion to form the flat-topped buttes and mesas of Monument Valley, Utah *(below).*

COASTLINES

THE COAST is a continuing battle between land and sea. Sometimes the sea "loses" as shingle, sand, or mud piles up and the land grows. In other places, the sea "wins" as waves, currents, and tides batter and break up the coast. Even hard rocks like granite are gradually worn away, especially during storms when high winds whip up huge waves powerful enough to smash pebbles and boulders against the shore.

The shape and features of a coastline depend on its rocks, winds, and currents. Very hard rocks erode slowly and stand out as high headlands. Waves blow at the shore with their greatest force in the direction of the main or prevailing winds in the region. Cliffs are sculpted both by the waves and by rockfalls and landslides. When waves undercut soft rocks, these collapse onto the shore and break up into tiny fragments. Wide beaches may eventually form, protecting the cliffs behind them from the full erosive force of the sea. A fast current may scour away broken rock particles from one part of the shore. As it slows down, it deposits them further along the coast as a mudflat, sand bar, or shingle spit.

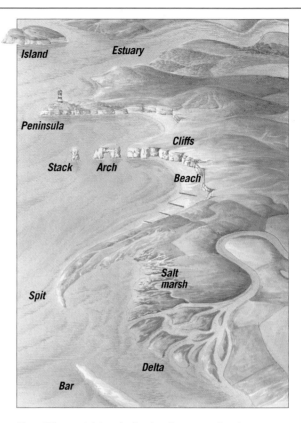

Along this coast *(above)* a hard rocky outcrop has become an island, cut off from the mainland by a flooded valley. Below the estuary, an arm of land is still linked to the mainland as a peninsula. A third outcrop has been wave-worn into an isolated pillar or stack, an arch and steep cliffs. Currents carry shingle from the bay's beach, slow down, and drop it to form a pointed spit and sand bar. Nearby, river mud is deposited to form a marshland and delta.

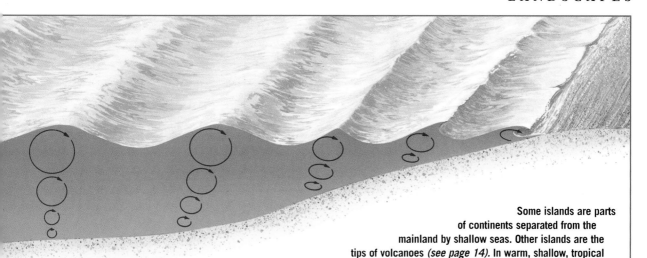

WAVES

As wind moves across the surface of the ocean, the water turns over and over in circles, forming waves. The wave itself moves along, but the water in a wave does not. It spins around in the same place and makes the water below turn, too. The height and power of a wave depend on the strength of the wind and the expanse of water it has blown across. In mid-ocean, large waves, called swell, can develop.

As a wave approaches the shallower seashore *(see illustration above),* the lower part drags on the sea bed, while the upper part travels on until, eventually, it topples over, or "breaks," on the shore.

Waves, particularly during a storm, can be powerful forces of erosion *(see page 18).* They cut away cliffs at the bottom, causing them to collapse. A headland may be attacked on both sides, becoming narrower and narrower. Joints and other weak areas are enlarged into sea caves. If caves form on either side of a headland, they may join up as a tunnel, later becoming a natural arch. If this collapses, a stack will result. This, too, eventually crumbles away over time.

In mountainous regions, valleys have been gouged out by glaciers *(see page 22).* They have a characteristic U-shape. In some parts of the world, most notably Norway and New Zealand, U-shaped valley near the coast have been "drowned" by rising sea levels. These deep inlets, known as fjords *(left),* have very steep sides. Some fjords snake inland for many miles.

Some islands are parts of continents separated from the mainland by shallow seas. Other islands are the tips of volcanoes *(see page 14).* In warm, shallow, tropical waters, billions of coral skeletons build up to form massive coral reefs around island coastlines *(below).* A volcano may eventually sink back into the ocean floor. Coral animals must stay near the light, so they build the reef taller, forming a circular barrier reef enclosing a lagoon containing the disappearing island. The volcano's tip may sink out of sight leaving a ring of coral islands—an atoll.

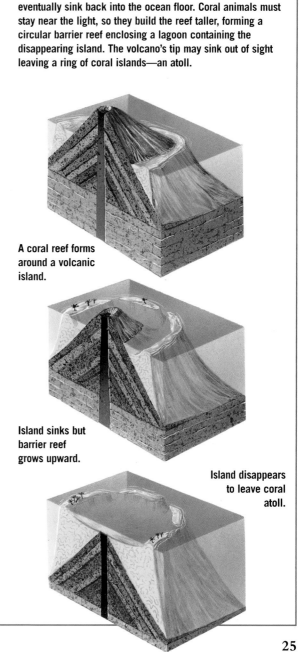

A coral reef forms around a volcanic island.

Island sinks but barrier reef grows upward.

Island disappears to leave coral atoll.

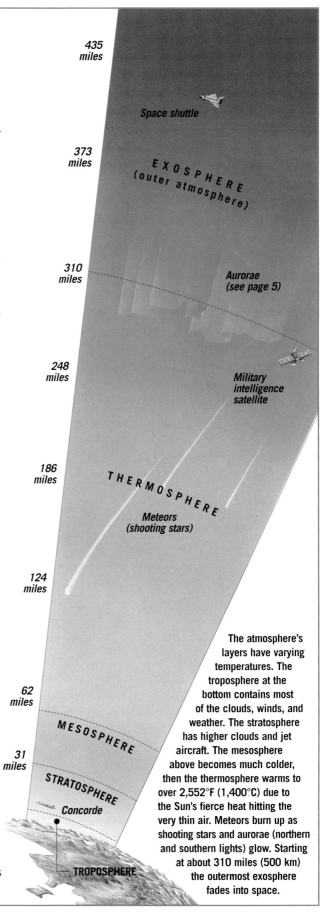

ATMOSPHERE

THE AIR we breathe is part of a thick blanket of air wrapped around Earth, known as the atmosphere. This air is a mixture of gases, mainly nitrogen (four-fifths) and oxygen (one-fifth). It gets thinner or less dense with height and fades away completely about 497 miles (800 km) above the ground, where the atmosphere ends and the nothingness of space begins.

The atmosphere has layers that rise and fall in temperature as the air gets thinner. The troposphere extends to 5.6 miles (9 km) high over the poles and 9.9 miles (16 km) above the equator. It is only one-seventieth of the atmosphere's total volume yet it contains four-fifths of all the air. Stratosphere temperature falls to −67°F (−55°C). The temperature rises to 50°F (10°C) at about 31 miles (50 km), where the mesosphere begins. It then plunges to a low of minus 167°F (75°C) at 49.7 miles (80 km), before rising again in the thermosphere.

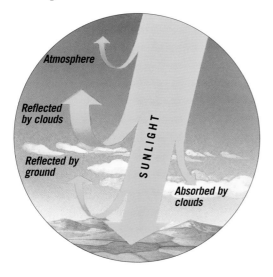

Atmosphere

Reflected by clouds

Reflected by ground

SUNLIGHT

Absorbed by clouds

The atmosphere not only provides us with oxygen to breathe. It shields us from the Sun's harmful rays. Some of these are reflected by various layers such as the stratosphere and the clouds *(above)*. Other rays have their energy absorbed and spread out through the atmosphere. The gas ozone occurs thinly in the stratosphere and absorbs most of the Sun's dangerous ultraviolet rays.

435 miles

Space shuttle

373 miles

EXOSPHERE
(outer atmosphere)

310 miles

Aurorae
(see page 5)

248 miles

Military intelligence satellite

186 miles

THERMOSPHERE

Meteors
(shooting stars)

124 miles

62 miles

MESOSPHERE

31 miles

STRATOSPHERE

Concorde

TROPOSPHERE

The atmosphere's layers have varying temperatures. The troposphere at the bottom contains most of the clouds, winds, and weather. The stratosphere has higher clouds and jet aircraft. The mesosphere above becomes much colder, then the thermosphere warms to over 2,552°F (1,400°C) due to the Sun's fierce heat hitting the very thin air. Meteors burn up as shooting stars and aurorae (northern and southern lights) glow. Starting at about 310 miles (500 km) the outermost exosphere fades into space.

SEASONS AND CLIMATE

IN TROPICAL REGIONS of Earth (around the middle or equator) it is hot all year round. Farther north the temperature varies through the year. It becomes warmer in spring, hot in summer, cool in autumn, and cold in winter. These time periods are called the seasons. They happen because of the way Earth goes around or orbits the Sun. Earth's orbit is not an exact circle around the Sun, but an ovallike ellipse. Also, the Earth spins each day around an imaginary line or axis going through the North and South Poles, but this axis is not at right angles to the orbit. It is tilted at an angle of 23.5°. The combination of tilted axis and elliptical orbit produce the yearly cycle of seasons in northern and southern regions.

At the middle of the year (1) Earth's top or northern half leans toward the Sun. The Sun is nearer and higher in the sky for longer each day so the north has summer. The southern half leans farther away from the Sun and days are shorter so it is winter. As Earth continues its orbit the tilt becomes sideways to the Sun (2), giving autumn in the north and spring in the south. At the year's end the southern half leans nearer the Sun and has summer while the north has winter (3), followed by southern autumn and spring in the north (4).

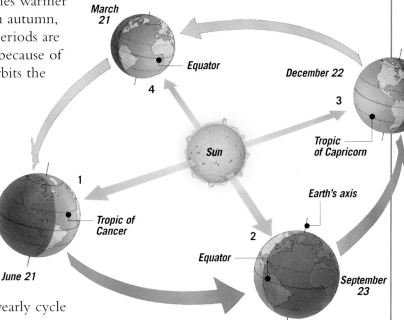

Winds result from uneven heating of different parts of the world. In the tropics, the surface is hot. This heats the air above it, which rises. Cooler air from the north and south blows in to replace it. These are called trade winds. Their direction is affected by Earth's spin.

Westerlies
Tropic of Cancer
Northeast trade winds
Equator
Southeast trade winds
Tropic of Capricorn
Westerlies

The map below shows the world's main climate regions. The Sun is nearest and highest in the sky over the tropical regions on either side of the equator. Also it shines directly down through the atmosphere here rather than at a low, slanting angle, so the atmosphere absorbs and scatters less of its heat. This is why tropical regions are hot all year. If dry winds blow over a tropical region they cause a tropical desert climate. At the top and bottom of Earth are polar regions where the Sun is farther away and lower in the sky, so these places are much colder. Between the topics and poles are temperate lands which have warm summer and cool winters.

Weather varies from day to day around the world *(see page 28)*. Over a longer period, especially many years, each region has a regular pattern of rain, wind, temperature, and other weather features. This long-term pattern of weather is called climate. It is due to the way Earth orbits the Sun *(top)* and the way that ocean currents and wind patterns *(above)* carry the Sun's warmth and rain-laden clouds around the globe.

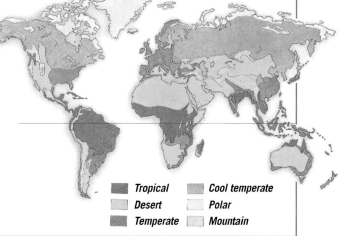

■ Tropical	■ Cool temperate	
■ Desert	■ Polar	
■ Temperate	■ Mountain	

WEATHER

WEATHER is the conditions and changes that take place in the lower atmosphere, up to about 12 miles (20 km) high. It includes temperatures by day and night, wind speed and direction, cloud type and cover, rain, hail, snow, frost, ice, droughts and storms. Weather can change by the minute or from day to day. The study of the weather is called meteorology.

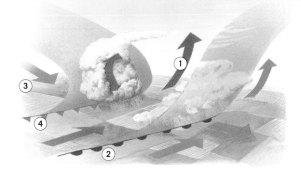

FRONTS

The driving force for our weather is the Sun. By day and night, winter and summer, it warms different parts of Earth's surface by different amounts. It evaporates water into the atmosphere to form clouds and also makes some regions of air warmer than others. Warm air rises and cooler air flows along to take its place, producing winds. When warm air (above, 1) flows up and over colder, heavier air, the moisture in it condenses, causing clouds to form and rain to fall. This is a warm front, shown on weather maps as a line with semicircles (2). When cold air (3) pushes against warm air along a cold front (4), it forms a low wedge, bringing a narrow band of heavy rain and then cooler, fresher, showery conditions.

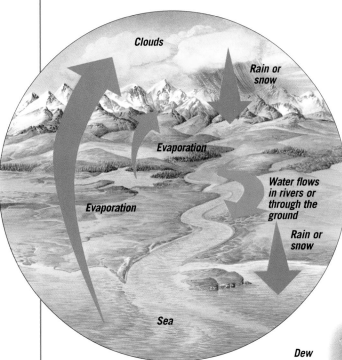

Clouds

Rain or snow

Evaporation

Water flows in rivers or through the ground

Rain or snow

Evaporation

Sea

Dew

WATER CYCLE

A vital part of weather and climate is the water cycle *(above)*. On our planet, water is not produced or destroyed—the same water goes round and round in an endless cycle. In rivers, lakes, and seas it is warmed by the Sun's heat. This evaporates or turns it into an invisible gas, water vapor. The warm water vapor rises high into the atmosphere where it is colder, so the vapor cools and condenses or turns back into liquid water. It forms tiny droplets or ice crystals floating as clouds. These merge, become bigger, and fall as rain or snow. The rain and melted snow flow into rivers, lakes, and seas—and the endless cycle continues.

Frost

DEW AND FROST

Water vapor is in the air around us, although we cannot see it. Sometimes it turns into liquid water or ice, which of course we can see. When the Sun goes down, the land cools faster than the air. Water vapor in the warmer air that touches the cooler land condenses. This covers everything with drops of water known as dew. If surface temperatures are below freezing, the water vapor turns into a layer of sparkling ice crystals called frost.

CLOUDS

A cloud is a vast gathering of billions of tiny water droplets, ice crystals, or a mixture of both *(below)*. They are so small and light that they float in the air. Clouds form at various heights above the ground and have different shapes *(right)*. The names describe these shapes using a combination of meanings. For example, cirrus is wispy or feathery, stratus is flat and blanketlike and cumulus is puffy and fluffy. Clouds form at ground level, too. We call them mist if they are thin and fog if they are thicker.

It is possible to forecast the weather from observing the different types of clouds. Highest at 32,808 feet (10 km) and above are cirrus, made of tiny ice crystals. Thin and wispy, they signal fine, dry, settled conditions. Cirrocumulus are small, regular-shaped clouds that look almost like fish scales and make a so-called mackerel sky. Altostratus and altocumulus form at medium heights and often mean that rain is on the way. Cumulus are the "cotton wool" clouds of a summer's day. Stratus are low clouds that cover the whole sky like a flat, pale gray sheet. Nimbostratus are even lower and usually bring heavy rain or snow.

The biggest and most impressive cloud is the cumulonimbus. It towers 16,404 feet (5,000 m) or more, with a fluffy white top and flat, gray "anvil" base. It usually brings fierce storms with thunder and lightning.

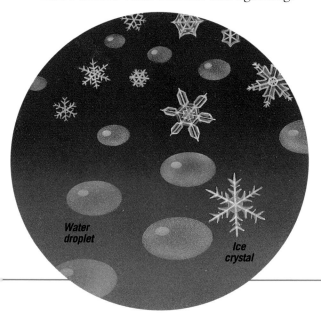

Water droplet

Ice crystal

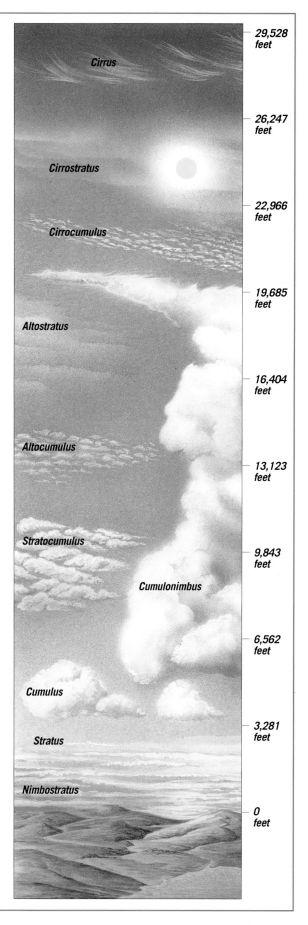

Cirrus — 29,528 feet

Cirrostratus — 26,247 feet

Cirrocumulus — 22,966 feet

Altostratus — 19,685 feet

— 16,404 feet

Altocumulus — 13,123 feet

Stratocumulus — 9,843 feet

Cumulonimbus

— 6,562 feet

Cumulus

— 3,281 feet

Stratus

Nimbostratus

0 feet

29

STORMS

THERE ARE many different kinds and sizes of storms. Most involve severe, violent weather with regions of high winds and heavy rain, and perhaps a sudden change in temperature. Some have thunder and lightning. They move across sea and land and may cause great damage and loss of life. Powerful winds blow down buildings and bridges and toss cars and trucks about like toys. Heavy rain or snow causes floods, mudslides, or avalanches.

Most storms begin as the Sun heats an area of land or sea and causes warm air to rise rapidly. Storms vary greatly in size and duration. A small tornado or "twister" may have a base just a few feet across and be gone in half an hour. A typical thunderstorm is 3–6 miles (5–10 km) wide and lasts for a few hours. A large hurricane may be more than 1,243 miles (2,000 km) across and rage on for two or three weeks.

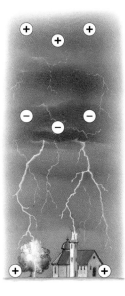

After hot, dry weather some parts of the land become very warm. As cool, moist air blows over them it is heated, rises fast, and cools. Its moisture turns into water droplets or ice crystals which form towering cumulonimbus clouds. The droplets and crystals swirl up and down inside the cloud. As they bump together, they become charged with static electricity. This builds up until it is suddenly released as a great spark of lightning. The heat of the flash makes the air around it expand so fast it makes a boom of thunder.

There are about 50,000 thunderstorms around the world every day. Each second, 100 bolts of lightning flash through clouds or down to the ground. A typical bolt has an electrical force of 100 million volts or more, and lasts one-fifth of a second. Thunderstorms often become more severe over cities because warm, moist air rises from the buildings and adds to their power.

Many storms are parts of cyclones. These are regions or centers of low air pressure around which winds blow. Because of the way Earth spins around, the winds blow counter-clockwise in the northern hemisphere and clockwise in the southern hemisphere. Near the equator, winds blowing around a tropical cyclone may increase in speed and tighten into a spiral to become a hurricane (known as a typhoon in the Pacific Ocean).

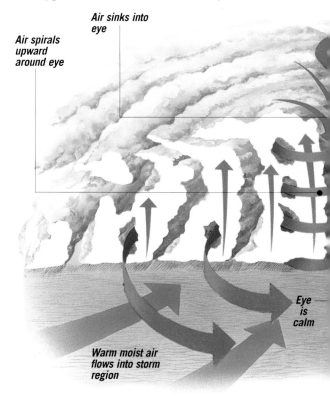

Air sinks into eye

Air spirals upward around eye

Eye is calm

Warm moist air flows into storm region

HURRICANES

Hurricanes begin as warm, moist air is heated by the fierce Sun and rises high into the atmosphere, usually over the western parts of the tropical Atlantic and Pacific Oceans. The rising air sucks in more air, which begins to swirl around in a spiral.

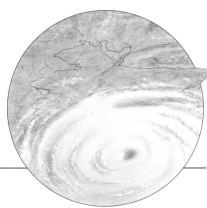

In 1970 a tropical cyclone (hurricane or typhoon) whipped up huge waves that surged over the low-lying mouth of the River Ganges in Bangladesh. Up to half a million people lost their lives.

Hurricanes may cause extensive damage. The winds roll cars, tip over planes, blow off roofs, and uproot trees. They also whip up great waves that pound the coast.

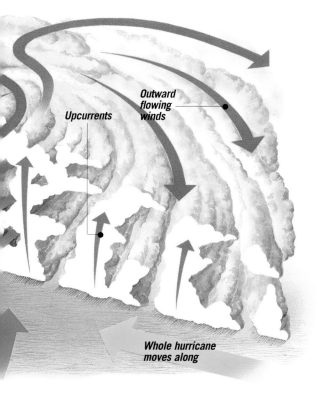

Upcurrents

Outward flowing winds

Whole hurricane moves along

TORNADOES

The fastest winds occur in the smallest storms—tornadoes. A tornado usually forms at the rear of a thundercloud as the winds swirl at 249 miles (400 km) per hour or more. A twisting column of air grows from the cloud like an upside-down funnel. Its base is only 67–328 feet (20–100 m) across. But the winds are so powerful that animals, people, cars, and even houses are plucked up into the clouds and then thrown outward. As the main storm moves at 25–50 miles (40–80 km) per hour the base may "skip" along the ground, doing the most damage when it touches down. Most tornadoes occur in the Midwestern United States, east of the Andes in South America, and in eastern India.

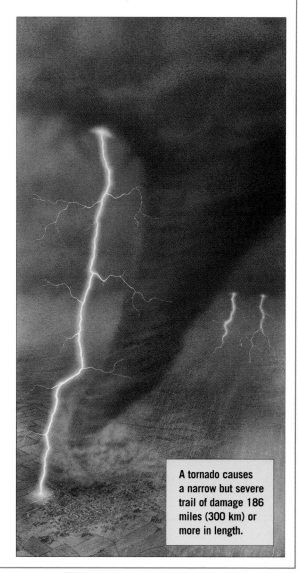

A tornado causes a narrow but severe trail of damage 186 miles (300 km) or more in length.

The moisture in the rising air condenses into clouds and begins to fall as heavy rain. Quickly the hurricane balloons in size and the swirling winds reach 155 miles (250 km) per hour. The spirals of deep cumulo-nimbus clouds unleash massive downpours, bringing up to half a year's average rainfall in a few hours. The hurricane moves along at 16–31 miles (25–50 km) per hour as warmed air rises and swirls most powerfully near its center. Most spills out at the top and is flung to the edges where it sinks. A small portion drifts down at the center or "eye" of the storm. This is usually 16–31 miles (25–50 km) across and, amazingly, it is calm with light winds and clear skies.

THE STORY OF THE EARTH

THE EARTH is 4,600 million years old. This huge span of time is difficult to imagine, so events in Earth's history are therefore measured in geological time, spans of millions of years. A "recent" event in geological time, for example, may have happened in the last million years.

Geologists divide time into three eons: the Archaean ("ancient"), from the origin of Earth to about 2500 million years ago (mya), the Proterozoic ("first life") to 530 mya, and the Phanerozoic ("visible life") to the present. The Archaean and Proterozoic are often referred to together as the Precambrian. The Phanerozoic is subdivided into eras: the Palaeozoic (530–250 mya), the Mesozoic (250–65 mya) and the Cenozoic (65 mya–present). The eras are split into periods, which are shown here *(right)*. The Tertiary and Quaternary periods are themselves divided into epochs.

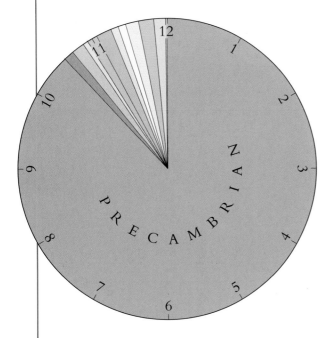

A way to understand geological time is to imagine 4,600 million years of Earth's history taking place in just 12 hours! The Precambrian would take up the first 10 ½ hours. From the Cambrian "explosion" of life *(see page 36)* to the present day would take up 90 minutes. The dinosaurs became extinct only 9 minutes ago. The entire history of humankind would make up the very last second.

million years ago	Period	Event
	QUATERNARY	First modern humans
1.8	TERTIARY	
65	CRETACEOUS	Dinosaurs extinct
		First flowering plants
144	JURASSIC	First birds
208	TRIASSIC	First mammals / First dinosaurs
250	PERMIAN	First archosaurs
286	CARBONIFEROUS	First mammal-like reptiles / First reptiles
360	DEVONIAN	First amphibians / First lobefin fish / First insects
408	SILURIAN	First fishes with jaws
438	ORDOVICIAN	First land plants / First jawless fishes
505	CAMBRIAN	First shellfish
530	PRECAMBRIAN	
3,500		Oldest fossils
4,600		Formation of Earth

The events of Earth's history are recorded in the rocks that formed at a certain time. When sediments such as sand, silt, or mud turned to rock *(see page 16),* the remains of life-forms that lived at the same time became fossilized *(see page 17)* in the same rocks. Thus scientists can piece together evidence of what the world was like in the various geological periods. Layers of sedimentary rock represent every geological epoch, although there is no place on Earth where rocks from every period in geological history are found.

DRIFTING CONTINENTS

The outer shell of Earth is divided up into large slabs, called tectonic plates *(see page 8).* These plates, which include both the continents and the floors of the oceans, move slowly at a rate of about 1 centimeter a year. Over geological time, entire continents have wandered around the globe, colliding into one another or drifting apart. About 200 million years ago, they came together to form a single "super-continent" called Pangaea. There was no Atlantic Ocean, and the Americas were jammed up against Africa and Europe. Since then, the continents have split apart, although some pieces, such as India and Asia, have collided with each other.

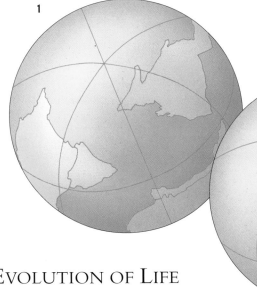

These three globes show the movement of the continents over geological time. Still widely separated 400 mya (1), they had collided to form Pangaea by 320 mya (2). They split apart during the Age of Dinosaurs, after 180 mya (3).

EVOLUTION OF LIFE

Scientists can work out when a particular animal or plant lived by establishing the age of the rocks in which its fossil was found. Over geological time, the fossil history tells us, animals (as well as other forms of life) have, very gradually, changed. Fins, tails, wings, or teeth may have developed as part of a process by which an animal adapts to its environment. This process is known as evolution, and plays a very important part in the course of Earth's history.

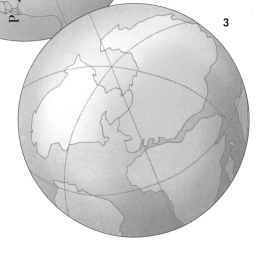

How do we know that continental drift has taken place? Fossils, once again, provide the evidence. The discovery of fossils of *Lystrosaurus (left),* a Triassic reptile, in South Africa, India, and Antarctica proves that these lands were once joined together (in Gondwanaland—*see page 42*). How else would this land animal have come to live in all three places?

THE ORIGIN OF THE EARTH

PLANET EARTH is one of nine planets orbiting the Sun, one of billions of stars in the Milky Way Galaxy, itself one of billions of galaxies in the universe. The universe came into existence 12–15 billion years ago. A few billion years later our galaxy was formed, but it was not until about 4,600 million years ago that the Sun and its family of planets, including Earth, made their appearance.

THE SOLAR SYSTEM FORMS

No one can say for sure how Earth was formed, but many scientists agree on a likely sequence of events. The solar system started out as a cloud of gas and dust drifting in space (many other such clouds in the galaxy are known to astronomers). Something—perhaps a series of shock waves emitted from a star exploding close by—caused the cloud to clump together under its own gravity. A huge, whirling disc of gas and dust was set in motion (1). Matter fell toward the center and became hotter and denser than at the edge of the disc. This core of intense energy was the beginnings of our sun.

   Meanwhile, the fragments of dust spinning around the core started to clump together, becoming at first small rocks, then "snowballing" into larger boulders, before growing into chunks several miles across, known as planetesimals. The planetesimals started to collide with one another, eventually building up to become the four rocky inner planets, Mercury, Venus, Earth, and Mars, and the rocky cores of the "gas giants," Jupiter, Saturn, Uranus, and Neptune. Energy from the Sun (the "solar wind") stripped away the gas that surrounded the inner planets (2). But the giant planets lay beyond the solar wind's fiercest blast and so held on to their thick atmospheres, which remain to this day.

YOUNG EARTH

In its early days, Earth was a barren planet, rather like the Moon is today. Unprotected by an atmosphere, it was continually bombarded by meteorites, millions of rocky fragments that careered around the youthful solar system. These crashed to the ground, some gouging out massive craters *(above left)*. The persistent bombardment may have caused Earth's rocky surface to melt: The planet became a global sea of extremely hot, molten rock *(above right and 3 opposite)*. Eventually the bombardment eased and the surface cooled. But the newly solidifed surface trapped gases beneath it.

The pressure built up and hydrogen, carbon dioxide, water vapor and nitrogen burst through the crust in volcanoes. Thousands of eruptions raged all over the globe *(below left and 4)*. The gases collected to form a new atmosphere around Earth. Water vapor rose to form the clouds that enveloped the planet (5).

Soon, as the Sun's intense heat began to cool, rain started to fall. It must have been the longest storm Earth has ever known. Water poured from the sky for many thousands of years until the basins in the land filled up, becoming the great oceans *(below right and 6)*.

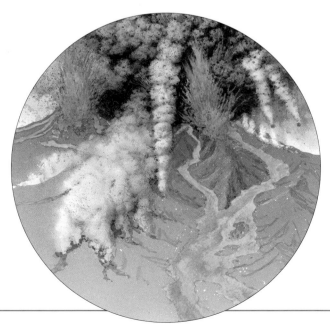

FIRST LIFE

THE FIRST LIFE on Earth appeared not on land but in the oceans. The atmosphere was still thin, so there was not enough oxygen in the air to sustain life. Ultraviolet radiation, lethal to life-forms, was also still at dangerous levels. Neither problem affected life underwater.

Life probably arose about 3,800 million years ago, although the earliest fossil evidence we have is 3,500 million years old. No one knows how life began, but scientists think that shallow, warm-water pools at the edges of the oceans would have been the ideal environment for the formation of chemicals that would eventually become the building blocks of life. The vital chemical reactions could have been triggered by lightning or the shock waves of a meteorite impact.

The earliest life-forms were the very simplest kinds—bacteria. The oldest fossils are known as stromatolites, bands of blue-green algae that grew in shallow water. It was another 2,500 million years before complex life forms, types of seaweed, first appeared.

The largest and fiercest of all Cambrian creatures was the 2 inch (60 cm) long *Anomalocaris,* a name meaning "odd shrimp". It had a cloaklike body, two large eyes set on stalks and a pair of pincerlike arms. Other smaller marine life-forms had defences to repel such giant marine predators. *Hallucigenia,* which moved about the sea bed on seven pairs of stilts, had a row of defensive spines on its back. *Wiwaxia* was hat-shaped, complete with two rows of daggerlike blades.

The first known animals existed from around 580 million years ago. Fossils of soft-bodied sea creatures, among them sea pens, jellyfish, worms, and crablike animals, found in the Ediacara Hills, Australia, give evidence of life in the Precambrian (already some five-sixths of the way through the story of Earth).

By about 530 million years ago, the first animals with hard parts—shells or bony skeletons—began to appear. Still confined to the sea, they included shellfish, corals, starfish, sponges and mollusks. Now a great variety of life-forms could be possible. This "explosion" of life took place at the beginning of the Cambrian Period. Fossils discovered in the Burgess Shale of British Columbia, Canada, show what the life in a warm, shallow sea in Cambrian times must have looked like. Among the life forms that we are familiar with today, there were some very strange-looking creatures. One, *Opabinia,* had five mushroomlike eyes and a long, clasping "nozzle" to catch prey.

KEY
1 *Opabinia*
2 *Anomalocaris*
3 *Pikaia*
4 *Leanchoilia*
5 *Aysheaia*
6 *Hallucigenia*
7 *Sanctacaris*
8 *Alalcomenaeus*
9 *Wiwaxia*

One of the Burgess Shale animals may be of particular significance to us. It is *Pikaia*, named after nearby Mt. Pika. This small, wormlike creature had a stiffening rod running the length of its body—not quite a backbone, but very similar to one. It also had muscles arranged in V-shaped segments, exactly the same as in modern fish. *Pikaia* may have been an early ancestor of the group of animals called vertebrates (animals with backbones) to which fish, reptiles, birds, and mammals such as ourselves all belong. Recent fossil finds from China show that fish, complete with gills but without jaws, swam in the oceans about 530 million years ago.

EARLY MARINE LIFE

THE CAMBRIAN Period was followed, 505 million years ago, by the Ordovician Period. Many species died out, to be replaced by new ones in another evolutionary "explosion." Trilobites first appeared in the Cambrian and rapidly became, for the next 250 million years, some of the most numerous of all kinds. Trilobites were members of the arthropod group, (creatures with a hard external skeleton and jointed limbs).

Arandapsis, an armored, jawless fish from the Ordovician Period.

Fish developed rapidly during the Silurian and Devonian Periods, evolving jaws, teeth, and fins. The evolution of jaws and teeth, allowed fish to become active predators. Fins gave them greater speed and maneuverability in the water. Two distinct types of fish emerged: those with skeletons made of soft cartilage (like the sharks and rays of today), and those that had hard, bony skeletons. This second group became dominant in late Devonian seas and rivers.

Some species with fleshy fins, called the lobefins, lived in warm waters in Devonian times, feeding on lakeside plants. One, a long, slender fish known as *Eusthenopteron,* developed lungs and could spend some time heaving itself around out of the water.

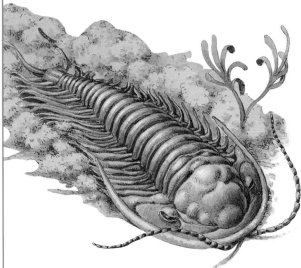

A trilobite's body was covered by a hard, jointed carapace (shield) divided into three lengthwise strips (its name means "three lobes"). Its legs allowed it to scuttle along the sea bed, or to paddle it through the water as it swam. Having no jaws, it used its legs to carry food to its mouth.

THE FIRST FISH

The first fish, perhaps descendants of *Pikaia (see page 37),* had "armor" plating to protect them from predators like the eurypterids. These were arthropods with large claws, some of which reached lengths of 6.5 feet (2 m). *Arandapsis,* known from fossils found in Australia, was one of the earliest. It fed by sucking in scraps of other dead animals floating in the water. Such fish dominated the seas for 130 million years.

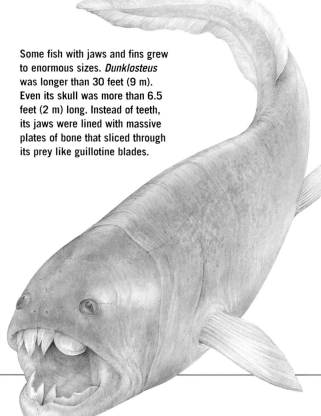

Some fish with jaws and fins grew to enormous sizes. *Dunklosteus* was longer than 30 feet (9 m). Even its skull was more than 6.5 feet (2 m) long. Instead of teeth, its jaws were lined with massive plates of bone that sliced through its prey like guillotine blades.

LIFE ON LAND

Until about 450 million years ago, there was no life on land. Blue-green algae may have been exposed to the air, or even washed ashore, at low tide. Very gradually, these minute plants may have acquired the means to stay alive longer on land. A waxy skin evolved to prevent them from drying out, followed by simple roots to anchor them in place. By the late Ordovician, plants had gained a foothold on land. By the end of the Silurian Period, plants had branching stems and water-conducting tubes *(above)*.

Land plants were a plentiful food source and certain marine animals evolved to take advantage of it. The arthropods' external skeletons were ideal protection against dehydration while out of the water. Their jointed legs allowed them to scuttle over uneven ground. Insects and spiders became the first land animals. They, in turn, were food for fish that lived near the water's edge. Gradually, lobefins like *Eusthenopteron* evolved the ability to "crawl" on their fins in pursuit of prey *(below)*. These fish may have been ancestors of the amphibians.

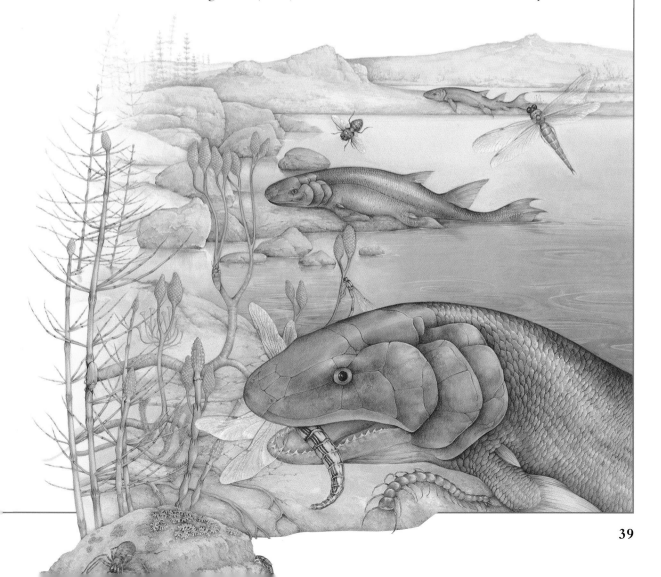

COAL SWAMPS

BY THE BEGINNING of the Carboniferous Period, plants had spread across the world's continents and had evolved into many different kinds, including massive trees. About 350 million years ago, Europe and North America were tropical lands. Hot, steamy jungles blanketed the lowlands. They are known as the coal swamps.

The continual cycle of growth and death of swampy vegetation produced thick layers of rotting matter that turned to peat, a dense, dark soil. Over millions of years, the thick beds of peat, overlain by sediments, were compressed, eventually becoming rock. This we know today as coal.

Massive trees, including *Lepidendron,* a kind of lycopod or club moss, and *Calamites,* a large horsetail, dominated the coal swamps. Dragonflies the size of pigeons, giant cockroaches, and 6.5 foot (2 m) long millipedes lived among the branches.

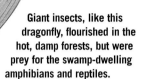

Giant insects, like this dragonfly, flourished in the hot, damp forests, but were prey for the swamp-dwelling amphibians and reptiles.

AMPHIBIAN TO REPTILE

Lurking in the waters of the Carboniferous coal swamps were the first amphibians. These animals had evolved from fish, their fins having become limbs with fingers and toes. *Ichthyostega,* an amphibian that lived in the tropics of Greenland (now a polar island), had a fishlike head and tail as it still spent time in the water, especially for the purpose of laying its jelly-covered eggs.

Eventually, some kinds of amphibian evolved a way of reproducing on land, thus avoiding the need to return to the water. Animals like tiny *Hylonomus* laid hard-shelled eggs. They were the first reptiles.

The Carboniferous seas also teemed with life. Sharks were the dominant predators. *Stethacanthus* had a strange, tooth-covered projection above its head.

A scene in North America about 300 million years ago. A group of *Eryops,* 6.5 feet (2 m) long amphibians, wade ashore among the dense vegetation of the coal swamp. These heavy, lumbering creatures probably spent most of their time in the water. Meanwhile, the 7.9 inch (20 cm) long *Hylonomus* ("forest mouse"), a lizardlike early reptile, looks on.

PERMIAN WORLD

DURING the Carboniferous period, Earth's two great continents, Laurasia (made up of parts of present-day Asia, North America, and Europe) and Gondwanaland (a combination of South America, Africa, Antarctica, and Australia) collided with one another, forming a single huge landmass. Geologists call this "supercontinent" Pangaea.

Much of southern Pangaea lay across the South Pole during the early Permian period. It was covered by an ice cap. A great deal of Earth's water was "locked up" in the ice. This meant that for the rest of the world the climate became very dry and hot.

The humid, tropical forests of the Carboniferous gave way to vast, dry scrub-lands and deserts. Large amphibians dependent on water for breeding started to die out, while reptiles multiplied. Their ability to lay eggs on land allowed them to live in dry environments. Besides strong legs and tough skin, they also developed powerful jaw muscles, which enabled them to eat tough desert plants.

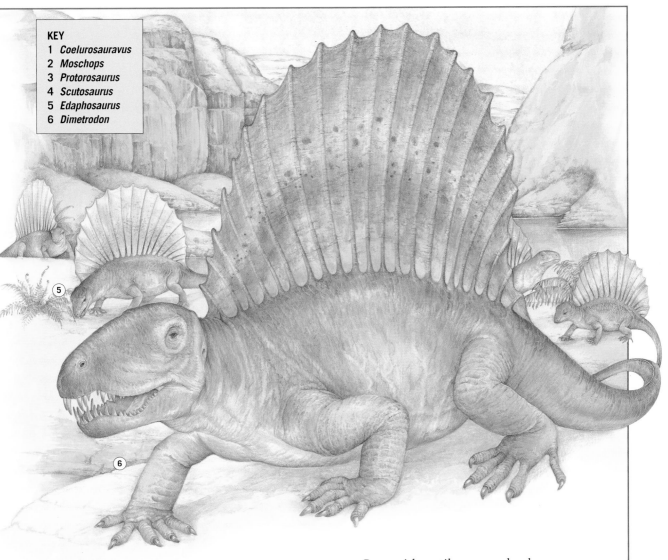

KEY
1 *Coelurosauravus*
2 *Moschops*
3 *Protorosaurus*
4 *Scutosaurus*
5 *Edaphosaurus*
6 *Dimetrodon*

AGE OF REPTILES

Reptiles of all kinds dominated the parched Permian world. (Some species, like *Mesosaurus,* adapted to life, once again, in the water. In future years, the strength and size of marine reptiles would make them fearsome predators.) Land reptiles could be classified into three groups, distinguished by openings in their skulls. The anapsids, fore-runners of turtles and tortoises, had none. The synapsids, which dominated the Permian landscape, had one opening on each side. Members of the third group, the diapsids, had two skull openings on each side. This group gave rise not only to modern lizards, snakes, and crocodiles, but also, in the Triassic period, to the dinosaurs.

Synapsid reptiles were also known as mammallike reptiles because they were the ancestors of the mammals. The earliest kinds to evolve were the pelycosaurs. Some, like *Dimetrodon* and *Edaphosaurus (above),* were 10 foot (3 m) long giants that had great sails on their backs. These were made of skin, supported by long thin spines sticking up from the backbone. It is thought that they may have acted as temperature regulators, the blood vessels in the skin quickly taking up, or giving off, the sun's heat.

The pelycosaurs were succeeded by the therapsids, a group that included the 16 foot (5 m) long, lumbering herbivore, *Moschops.* Equally slow-moving was the anapsid *Scutosaurus.* Diapsids were still quite scarce. They included *Coelurosauravus,* a tiny glider, and fast-moving *Protorosaurus.*

TRIASSIC WORLD

THE TRIASSIC PERIOD began at a time, 250 million years ago, when a vast number of animals, both on land and in the sea, became extinct. Scientists are unsure why, although the extreme hot and dry climatic conditions across the continent of Pangaea may have been responsible.

A number of reptiles survived the extinctions, however, including the mammallike reptiles. *Lystrosaurus,* a tusked, piglike reptile, spread rapidly *(see page 33).* Another group of reptiles began to achieve dominance at this time. With their powerful jaws and bony armor, the archosaurs, from the diapsid group, quickly multiplied. Early archosaurs had a low, sprawling gait (like modern lizards), but, as the Triassic went on, some kinds began to stand more upright. The powerful runner *Ornithosuchus,* for example, had a short body with a long, counterbalancing tail and strong hind legs. By the late Triassic, some archosaur species moved around on two legs all the time. They were the first dinosaurs.

Euparkeria was an archosaur, a forerunner of the dinosaurs. It could run on its hind legs.

THE FIRST DINOSAURS

The first known dinosaurs appeared about 230 million years ago in the southern part of South America and in southern Europe. In Triassic times, both these regions lay on the fringes of Pangaea, a lush landscape—in contrast to the supercontinent's arid interior. These early dinosaurs were small theropods (meat eaters) which ran on two legs. *Herrerasaurus,* from South America, had a flexible neck, large eyes, sharp teeth, and a long tail, which acted as a balance. Its strong back legs left its arms free to grasp its prey.

South America in the Triassic period.

KEY
1 *Riojasaurus*
2 *Herrerasaurus*
3 *Mussaurus*

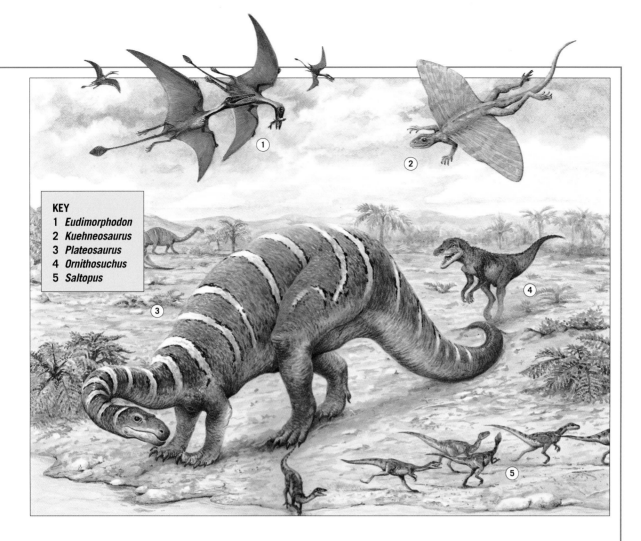

KEY
1 *Eudimorphodon*
2 *Kuehneosaurus*
3 *Plateosaurus*
4 *Ornithosuchus*
5 *Saltopus*

The plant eaters, or sauropods, emerged later, toward the end of the Triassic. One of the largest of the early sauropods was the 33 foot (10 m) long *Riojasaurus,* also from south America. Another was *Plateosaurus,* from Europe *(above).* Twenty-six feet (8 m) long, it probably spent most of its time on all fours but, on occasions, its long, powerful back legs allowed it to rear up to feed from the tops of trees, or even to run short distances on two legs. *Plateosaurus* may have used its large, curved thumb claw to pull down branches. Unable, like many dinosaurs, to chew its food, it swallowed stones which ground up tough plants inside its stomach, making them easier to digest.

Not all plant eaters were so enormous. *Mussaurus* was from South America. Its name, meaning "mouse lizard," was given to it because the first skeleton to be discovered was tiny. Scientists later realized that this skeleton was actually that of a baby. Adults grew to be 10 feet (3 m) long.

One of the best known of all Triassic dinosaurs was *Coelophysis*. A 10 foot (3 m) long theropod, it lived in what is now the southern United States. *Coelophysis* had a long, narrow head and sharp, saw-edged teeth, which it used to devour lizards and other small prey. Large numbers of fossils have been found together, suggesting that *Coelophysis* lived in packs like wolves. Some skeletons contained the bones of their young, suggesting that these dinosaurs might have been cannibals.

Coelophysis was a slender-bodied dinosaur, built for speed.

JURASSIC WORLD

DURING JURASSIC times, from 208 to 144 million years ago, the super-continent of Pangaea began to split in two: Laurasia and Gondwanaland started to drift apart again. The climate, while still warm, became much wetter. Sea levels rose, causing widespread flooding of low-lying lands. Plants, especially coniferous trees, became abundant, providing a rich food source for the dinosaurs, now the only large land-living animals.

The sauropods evolved into larger and larger kinds, culminating in such giants as *Diplodocus* and *Brachiosaurus,* among the longest and largest land animals that have ever lived. These enormous creatures, measuring more than 65 feet (20 m) long, had very long necks and equally long, whiplike tails to balance them. Their teeth, shaped like pegs (in *Diplodocus* and *Brachiosaurus*) or spoons (in *Cetiosaurus* and *Camarasaurus*), were perfectly designed for tearing off leaves from trees.

As the sauropods became larger and more numerous, so the meat eating theropods became more powerful hunters, capable of bringing down a 65 foot long (20 m)

Stegosaurus was a plant-eating dinosaur. It may have been able to rear up on its back legs to feed from trees.

sauropod, either individually or hunting in packs. *Megalosaurus,* from Jurassic Europe, was about 30 feet (9 m) long. Equipped with powerful jaws, it was able to attack even quite large sauropods. (*Megalosaurus* was the first dinosaur to be discovered and, in 1824, to be given a name.) Top predator in North America at the same time was 39 foot (12 m) long *Allosaurus.* It may have hunted in packs to attack *Diplodocus.* Any prey trapped in its backward-curving teeth would have found it hard to escape.

KEY
1 *Cetiosaurus*
2 *Megalosaurus*
3 *Echinodon*
4 *Compsognathus*

To defend themselves against these fearsome predators, some plant eaters developed armor. *Stegosaurus,* a 33 foot (10 m) long, slow-moving dinosaur from North America, had a double row of diamond-shaped bony plates running the length of its back. It also possessed several long spines at the end of its tail, with which it could lash out at its attacker.

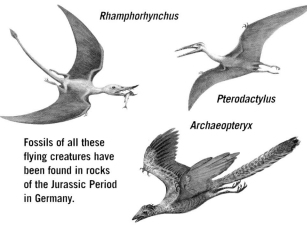

Rhamphorhynchus

Pterodactylus

Archaeopteryx

Fossils of all these flying creatures have been found in rocks of the Jurassic Period in Germany.

Alongside the massive Jurassic dinosaurs lived some of the smallest dinosaurs known. No bigger than a cat, *Compsognathus* was a long-legged, fast-moving predator, feeding on lizards and other small creatures it chased through the undergrowth. Fossils of its skeleton show that it had a very similar build to *Archaeopteryx,* one of the earliest-known birds, which lived in the same region, Europe, and at the same time, 150 million years ago, as *Compsognathus.* Recent evidence that some dinosaurs may have been feathered supports the belief that birds are descended from dinosaurs.

The birds were not the first vertebrates to fly, however. Flying reptiles, known as pterosaurs, had first taken to the air millions of years earlier during the Triassic period. *Rhamphorhynchus* and *Pterodactylus* were marine predators in the Jurassic.

Sheets of skin between the fourth finger and the body made up a pterosaur's wings, Many had powerful, toothed beaks that were perfect for seizing, and holding onto, fish they caught while skimming the surface of the sea.

The Jurassic saw the emergence of a new kind of dinosaur. The sauropods and theropods were saurischian, or lizard-hipped, dinosaurs: Their hip bones were shaped like those of other reptiles. Now a new group, the ornithischians, or bird-hipped dinosaurs, made their appearance. Their hip bones were shaped like those of modern birds (although, confusingly, birds were themselves descended from the saurischian kind). Equipped with the ability to chew their food, these plant eaters quickly multiplied, taking advantage of the ever-increasing variety of plants found in the late Jurassic environment.

Brachiosaurus is the largest dinosaur known from a complete fossil skeleton. At 46 feet (14 m) tall, it would have been able to look into the top-floor window of a four-story building! It used its long neck to tear leaves from high in the trees.

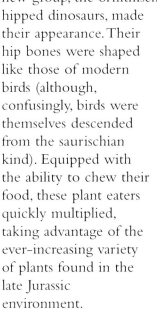

Human being (at same scale)

KEY
1 *Nothosaurus*
2 *Placodus*
3 *Henodus*

MARINE REPTILES

WHILE the dinosaurs ruled the land and the pterosaurs circled in the skies, reptiles also dominated the seas. Some kinds of reptile began to feed on marine life during the Triassic period, and gradually the body design of marine reptiles adapted to an underwater lifestyle.

One of the earliest marine reptiles, *Placodus,* lived in shallow coastal waters. Apart from its long, fishy tail, it looked very much like a land reptile, with its short neck, heavy body and sprawling legs. It used its powerful jaws to crush shellfish. Long-necked *Nothosaurus* was a more streamlined swimmer, spending its time resting on land and feeding in the water in the same way that seals do today. *Henodus* was quite similar to a modern turtle. Its bony-plated shell protected it from attack by predators. A toothless beak was designed for breaking open shellfish.

The best-adapted ocean reptiles were the ichthyosaurs, such as *Ichthyosaurus (below)*. They were at their most abundant during the Jurassic period, a time when shallow, warm seas covered much of Earth. Like modern dolphins, ichthyosaurs were perfectly streamlined, with long flippers for steering and strong tails to propel them through the water. They were the first marine reptiles to spend all of their time in the water. They gave birth to live young.

The Jurassic period saw the emergence of another important group of marine reptiles—the plesiosaurs. Like dinosaurs, they had long necks and small heads. Instead of legs, their limbs had become large, paddlelike flippers which they used like underwater "wings" to pull themselves through the water, beating in a slow, steady rhythm. Plesiosaurs fed on fish and squid, darting their long, flexible necks backward and forward to pick off their prey. They spent most of their time in the water, coming ashore only to lay their eggs.

By the late Cretaceous, some plesiosaurs had become giants. *Elasmosaurus* was 46 feet (14 m) long—with a neck more than half its body length. It could have held its head clear of the water, hunting for prey from a high vantage point *(below)*.

Giant pterosaurs and plesiosaurs scour the seas for prey in this Cretaceous scene.

CRETACEOUS WORLD

THE CRETACEOUS PERIOD was the heyday for the dinosaurs. Laurasia and Gondwanaland, the northern and southern halves of Pangaea, themselves started to break up into smaller landmasses. These would later become the continents we know today. The climate remained as warm and humid as in Jurassic times, and a wide variety of plant life grew in all parts of the world—including Antarctica, today a frozen wasteland. Flowering plants, including deciduous trees, which had evolved during the Jurassic, replaced some more ancient plant species.

The abundance of plant food favored new kinds of ornithischians. They became more abundant during the early Cretaceous, while many of the massive, long-necked sauropods, such as *Brachiosaurus* and *Apatosaurus,* died out. Unlike the slow, lumbering sauropods, many of these new kinds were small, fast-moving dinosaurs. Like gazelles, when danger threatened, a herd of *Hypsilophodon,* from Cretaceous Europe, would sprint for safety.

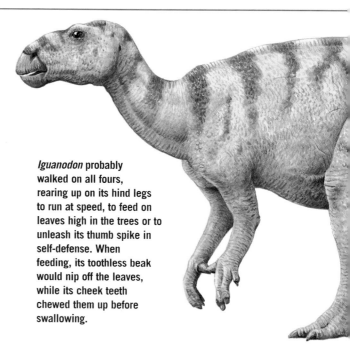

Iguanodon probably walked on all fours, rearing up on its hind legs to run at speed, to feed on leaves high in the trees or to unleash its thumb spike in self-defense. When feeding, its toothless beak would nip off the leaves, while its cheek teeth chewed them up before swallowing.

IGUANODON

Iguanodon, a considerably larger animal 30 feet (9 m) long, was much less nimble than *Hypsilophodon,* relying instead on another means of defense. As well as its clawed fingers, *Iguanodon* had a large, viciously sharp thumb spike, which it could have jabbed into the neck of any predatory dinosaur. Herds of *Iguanodon* roamed tropical forests the world over.

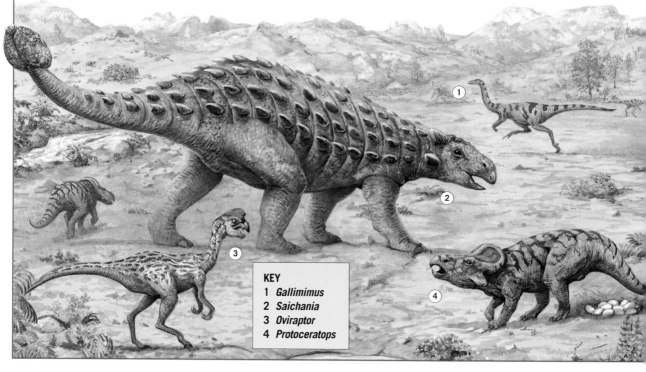

KEY
1 *Gallimimus*
2 *Saichania*
3 *Oviraptor*
4 *Protoceratops*

CRETACEOUS CARNIVORES

During Cretaceous times, a variety of new predatory dinosaurs appeared, some very large, like *Carnotaurus,* and some relatively small, like the dromaeosaurs. Hunting in packs, *Deinonychus,* a 10 foot (3 m) long dromaeosaur from North America could bring down larger prey using its hooked, slashing foot claws. Other predators included the ornithomimids, intelligent, fast-running hunters of small prey, and the giant tyrannosaurs *(see page 52).*

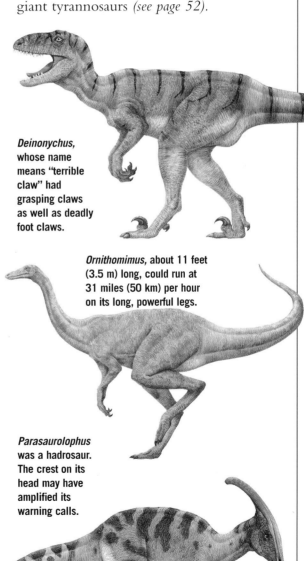

Baryonyx (below) was an unusual theropod dinosaur from Cretaceous Europe. It had the body of a large carnivore 20 feet (6 m) long, but its skull was long and narrow, with many small, sharp teeth—more like that of a crocodile. *Baryonyx* probably fed on fish, wading through the shallows and hooking out its prey with its long thumb claw, after which it is named ("heavy claw").

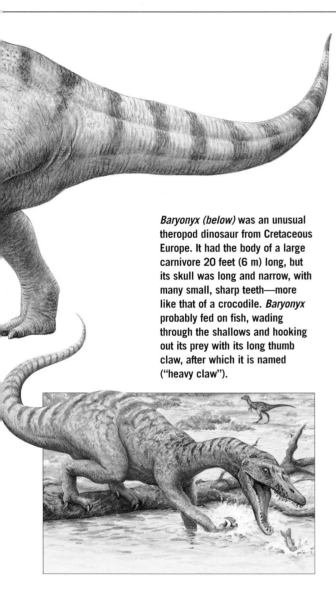

Deinonychus, whose name means "terrible claw" had grasping claws as well as deadly foot claws.

Ornithomimus, about 11 feet (3.5 m) long, could run at 31 miles (50 km) per hour on its long, powerful legs.

Parasaurolophus was a hadrosaur. The crest on its head may have amplified its warning calls.

OTHER HERBIVORES

The Cretaceous period also saw the emergence of the hadrosaurs, ornithischian dinosaurs that had cheek teeth which continually replaced old, worn ones. It enabled them to take full advantage of the plentiful vegetation that grew in late Cretaceous times.

Armored dinosaurs also evolved many different forms. The ankylosaurs were formidable, tanklike dinosaurs, covered with rows of hard, bony plates and spikes. If this were not enough to deter an attacker, ankylosaurs like *Saichania,* from Mongolia, had a large ball of bone at the end of their tails which they could swing like clubs.

THE END OF THE DINOSAURS

Megazostrodon was one of the first mammals. It was an insect eater, just (5 cm) long.

BY THE END of the Cretaceous period, about 65 million years ago, all the dinosaurs were extinct. They had ruled the land for more than 160 million years (by comparison, anatomically modern humans have existed for just 125,000 years). Although birds and mammals had evolved during the Age of Dinosaurs, no other large land creatures, save crocodiles, which spent most of their time in rivers, existed.

The last years of the dinosaurs produced some of the most spectacular kinds. Of the plant eaters, the hadrosaurs, such as *Lambeosaurus* and *Pachycephalosaurus,* were very numerous, but they were joined by a new group, the ceratopians, the horned dinosaurs. In North America, for the last 20 million years or so of the dinosaurs' reign, they were the most abundant large herbivores on Earth. Animals like the 30 foot (9 m) giant *Triceratops* had a huge skull, a massive neck frill for self-defense long horns and a parrotlike beak.

Only the largest, most powerful predator would have been a match for *Triceratops.* Unfortunately for *Triceratops,* just such a monster existed: *Tyrannosaurus rex.* This awesome, 39 foot (12 m) long killing machine had massive powerful back legs which gave it great speed over short distances. It had an enormous head, with jaws surrounded by rows of saw-edged teeth, some up to 7 inches (18 cm) long. Only its arms were puny, but had they been longer, the dinosaur would have over balanced. *Tyrannosaurus* probably made its kill by charging its prey, bringing it down with devastating bites. It may also have scavenged the kills of others.

MASS EXTINCTION

The dinosaurs, the pterosaurs, all marine reptiles and a large number of other species all died out at the end of the Cretaceous. No one yet knows why this was so, but the evidence shows that the event was quite abrupt. It is thought by some scientists that a massive asteroid (a large rocky object in space) may have crashed into Earth *(above)*. The resulting explosion may have filled the atmosphere with dust, blotting out the sun and lowering temperatures for years on end.

A *Tyrannosaurus* and *Triceratops* confront one another in North America 70 million years ago. Although *Triceratops's* neck frill gave it some protection from attack, the teeth of *Tyrannosaurus* were sharp enough to penetrate the herbivore's scaly skin.

By another theory, a massive volcanic eruption could have taken place on Earth, blasting millions of cubic miles of lava into the atmosphere, producing the same effect on the climate as an asteroid collision.

Evidence for both theories comes from the discovery by geologists of a layer of metal, called iridium, in late Cretaceous rocks. This metal is believed to be present in the core of Earth and in asteroids, but nowhere else. Iridium dust thrown up by an exploding asteroid or lava from inside Earth may have settled on the surface, then later compacted in the rocks of the time.

Small mammals explore the skeleton of a *Triceratops*. The Age of Dinosaurs is over.

SURVIVORS

While the dinosaurs and others perished, a number of reptile species survived the extinction, including lizards, snakes, crocodiles, and turtles. But the disappearance of the dinosaurs and pterosaurs offered an opportunity for mammals to become the dominant land animals, and for birds to rule supreme in the air.

Mammals had evolved from mammallike reptiles back in the Triassic period, 225 million years ago. They had fur on their skins, enabling them to become warm-blooded. But, while dangerous dinosaur predators were about, they remained tiny, shrewlike animals venturing out only at night to feed. Their time had now come.

THE AGE OF MAMMALS

AFTER THE DRAMATIC extinctions at the end of the Cretaceous period, Earth entered what is known as the Tertiary period. It is divided into a number of epochs *(see page 32)* beginning with the Palaeocene and finishing 1.8 million years ago as the Ice Age dawned.

By the beginning of the Tertiary, the continents had drifted to approximately their present positions, although North and South America were still separated. Each continent, with the exception of Australia and Antarctica which were still linked together, had become an isolated landmass. This meant that early mammals evolved separately on their own island continent.

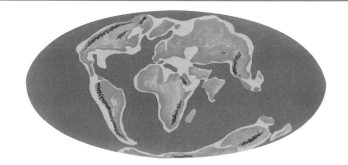

This is a map of the world during Eocene times (part of the Tertiary period), about 50 million years ago *(above)*. The pale blue areas are shallow seas, tracts of land that have been submerged beneath high sea levels.

This is what a region of North Africa, today barren desert, would have looked like 35 million years ago *(below)*. Living in the swamps were the early elephant *Phiomia*, the rhinoceros-like *Arsinoitherium* and a primitive ape *Aegyptopithecus*.

KEY
1 *Aegyptopithecus*
2 *Arsinoitherium*
3 *Phiomia*

By the time the dinosaurs became extinct, several different groups of mammals had already evolved around the world. During the Palaeocene and early Eocene epochs, the climate was warm and tropical rain forest was widespread, even at the poles. Mammals that were best suited to moving through dense trees dominated.

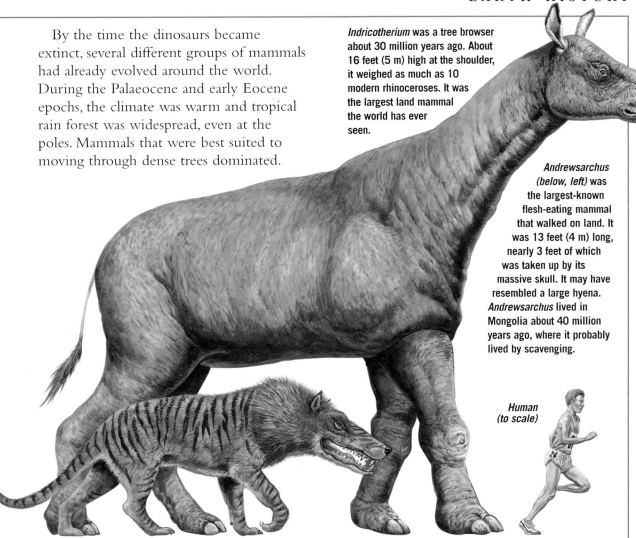

Indricotherium was a tree browser about 30 million years ago. About 16 feet (5 m) high at the shoulder, it weighed as much as 10 modern rhinoceroses. It was the largest land mammal the world has ever seen.

Andrewsarchus (below, left) was the largest-known flesh-eating mammal that walked on land. It was 13 feet (4 m) long, nearly 3 feet of which was taken up by its massive skull. It may have resembled a large hyena. *Andrewsarchus* lived in Mongolia about 40 million years ago, where it probably lived by scavenging.

Human (to scale)

ROOTERS AND BROWSERS

The mammals of the Palaeocene were forest dwellers. They included a number of species that look unfamiliar to us today. Some roamed the forest floor seeking plant stems or roots. They included the strange, knobbly headed *Uintatherium* or twin-horned *Arsinoitherium*. Others, such as rodents and primates, browsed for leaves and fruits in the trees themselves.

No large carnivorous mammals then existed. But among the birds, which had also developed into a wide variety of species, were some predatory giants—for example, the 10 foot (3 m) high, ground-dwelling *Diatryma* from North America. With its enormous, bone-crushing beak, *Diatryma* feasted on mammals, including even small, primitive horses!

MAMMAL GIANTS

During the Oligocene epoch, the climate began to cool. Ice caps formed at the poles and many dense forests were replaced by more open woodland. The forest dwellers gave way to much larger mammals that thrived in these conditions. They included *Indricotherium,* a massive rhinoceros from Central Asia, and *Andrewsarchus,* an early mammalian carnivorous giant.

By the Miocene, vast areas of grassland had opened up, leading to the evolution of fast-running horses and antelopes, as well as predatory dogs, cats, and hyenas. Massive elephants, adapted to feeding from trees on grasslands, evolved. Meanwhile, some fish-eating carnivores developed the ability to spend more time in the water, and evolved into the group we now call the whales.

THE ICE AGES

THE QUARTERNARY period runs from about 1.8 million years ago to the present. The Pleistocene epoch, which occupies all but the last 10,000 years, was the time of the Ice Age, during which, on at least four occasions, great ice sheets spread southward and buried much of northern Europe, North America, and Asia. In between, there were periods of warmer, even subtropical, climate, called interglacials.

Coelodonta, the Ice Age woolly rhinoceros.

The Pleistocene Ice Age is not the only one in the history of the Earth. A major ice age occurred in the late Carboniferous and early Permian periods, about 290 million years ago *(see page 42)*. Today's climates are generally cooler than on many occasions in prehistory, so it is quite possible that we are living through an interglacial. A fifth ice age may one day grip the world.

It is not clear what causes an ice age. It may be that Earth's angle of rotation changes slightly, tipping the poles further away from the sun's rays *(see page 27)*

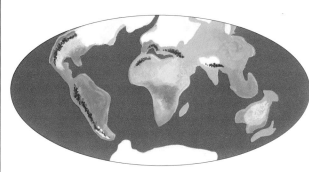

This is a map of the world as it was 40,000 years ago, at the height of the last Ice Age during the Pleistocene epoch. The white areas show the ice caps. Today, ice caps cover the Arctic Ocean, Greenland and some of the islands of northern Canada. During the Ice Age, ice caps stretched much further south. The ice "locked up" a great deal of the world's water, resulting in lower sea levels.

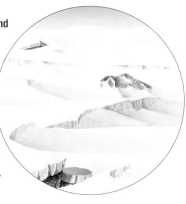

Most of North America and northern Europe looked like this 40,000 years ago. The ice was 1.9 miles (3 km) thick in places. The advancing ice gouged out valleys, smoothed over hills and plains and filled rock basins with water, forming lakes, when they melted.

Gigantopithecus was a massive ape, standing about 8 feet (2.5 m) tall. It roamed the forests of China in Ice Age times, feeding on leaves. Some say this ape is the origin of the Yeti legend.

The Ice Age had a major effect on the world's climate, and its wildlife experienced major changes, too. During the warmer interglacials, animals like elephants, hippopotamuses, and hyenas could migrate northward. When the ice sheets spread southward, mammoths, rhinoceroses, reindeer, and bears adapted to life in the vast regions of tundra, treeless areas of low grasses and frozen soils. Some migrated south in winter, others hibernated.

Mammoths are the best-known Ice Age mammals. Woolly mammoths *(below),* with their shaggy coats and layers of body fat, were well suited to the cold, summerless environments of the north. They roamed the northern tundra lands until about 10,000 years ago (although a small number survived on a Siberian island until just 3,500 years ago). Complete carcasses, preserved in ice, are still found today. Climatic change probably finished them, but they may have been hunted to extinction by humans.

HUMAN EVOLUTION

Humanlike animals, called hominids, first appeared about four million years ago, but the evolution of modern human beings took place during the Ice Age. The fossil evidence points to the grasslands of Africa being our place of origin, from where humans spread out to all parts. One branch of the *Homo sapiens* family, called Neanderthals, adapted to the cold European climate, but died out 30,000 years ago.

FUTURE EARTH

THE EARTH is 4,600 million years old and is expected to have a natural life of another 5,000 million years. What will the future hold? Living things, in one form or another, have existed for at least 3,500 million years, undergoing constant change and evolution. What will future living things be like? How long will humans survive?

In the short term, the one thing scientists are agreed upon is that Earth will become much warmer. This is known as global warming. The average temperature has risen by more than 32.9°F (0.5°C) in the past century. This is predicted to rise to 35.6°F (2°C) by 2050. The effects may be felt as more violent storms, shifting rainfall patterns, and rising seas, which could submerge many of the world's coastal areas. Many scientists believe that the the emission of certain gases—chlorofluorocarbons (CFCs), carbon dioxide, and methane— from factories, cars, and power stations may contribute to the "greenhouse effect" *(above right),* a likely reason for the rise in global temperatures.

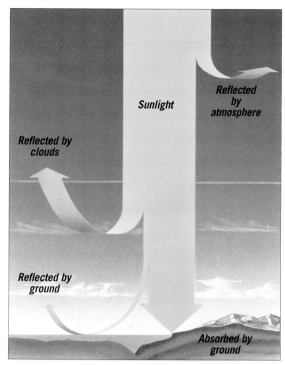

Earth's surface and its clouds both absorb sunlight, before releasing it back into space. Some gases trap part of this outgoing heat in the atmosphere, keeping the surface warm—just like a greenhouse. Increasing levels of these so-called greenhouse gases may warm the Earth too much.

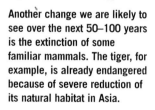

Another change we are likely to see over the next 50–100 years is the extinction of some familiar mammals. The tiger, for example, is already endangered because of severe reduction of its natural habitat in Asia.

Volcanic eruptions occur all over the Earth. Occasionally, a major eruption may throw up so much material into the atmosphere that the climate is affected. This could have led to the extinction of the dinosaurs. Could it happen to us?

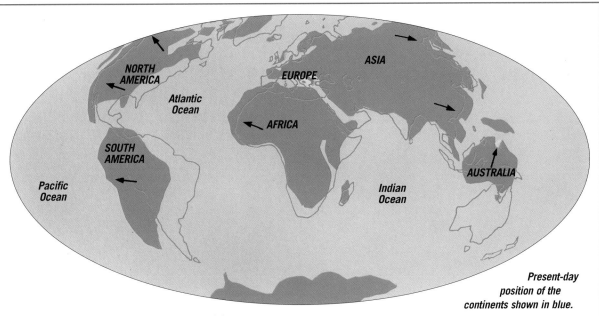

Present-day position of the continents shown in blue.

This is how the world may look 50 million years from now. The Atlantic Ocean has spread apart. North and South America are no longer joined together and Africa and Asia have split at the Red Sea. Australia has collided with Indonesia.

In the longer term—millions of years into the future—Earth itself will continue to change. Rivers and glaciers will erode upland areas, creating new lowlands. These may then be uplifted, creating, in turn, new uplands. The continents will go on drifting around the globe, creating or destroying landmasses and ocean floors. Despite the probable destruction of a number of living environments by humans, life will go on evolving.

How will humankind cope with this change? The reduction of greenhouse gases, by a switch to alternative forms of energy, could arrest global warming. A new approach to conservation may save some well-known species from immediate extinction. In the longer term, it would seem very little could save our planet from an asteroid impact or cataclysmic volcanic eruption. The search for new planets to inhabit may provide a safe haven for people to survive such a catastrophe.

The discovery of new planets around other stars raises the possibility that we might one day encounter life from other worlds. Will extraterrestrial life-forms look like this, the popular idea of an alien? What will be the impact on us and our planet?

The impact of a large asteroid colliding with Earth would be catastrophic. Over millions of years, it is bound to happen.

GLOSSARY

Abyssal plain A flat region of the ocean floor, covered by a thick layer of mud and other sediments.

Archosaurs A group of reptiles that first appeared in the late Permian period and gave rise to the crocodiles, pterosaurs, dinosaurs, and birds.

Arthropods Animals without backbones but with an external skeleton. They include insects, crustaceans, spiders, and millipedes.

Atmosphere The blanket of gases surrounding Earth that enables life to exist.

Aurora (plural: aurorae) The display of colored lights seen in the night skies close to Earth's poles. It occurs when high-energy particles from the Sun are trapped by Earth's magnetic field.

Condensation The process by which a gas becomes liquid.

Continental drift The movement of continents around the globe. Earth's outer layer is made up of separate tectonic plates, which are constantly grinding into, away from, or alongside one another, taking continents or parts of continents with them.

Continental shelf The part of a continent that lies beneath ocean waters.

Continental slope The steep part of the continental shelf that plunges down to the abyssal plain.

Convection current The movement of heat through liquids and gases. Heated from below, a liquid or gas will expand, become less dense, and rise. Away from the source of heat, the opposite will occur, and the liquid or gas will fall.

Core The innermost portion of Earth.

Crust The thin, rocky outer layer of Earth. There are two main types of crust: continental and oceanic.

Desert An area of very low rainfall

Dinosaurs Reptiles that lived on land during the Mesozoic era (250–65 million years ago) and which walked upright on legs held beneath their bodies, like birds and mammals.

Earthquake A shaking or trembling of the ground, caused by the sudden movement of part of Earth's crust.

Erosion The wearing away of Earth's surface by water, ice, or wind.

Evaporation The process by which a liquid becomes gas.

Evolution The process by which forms of life have changed over millions of years, gradually adapting to make the best use of their environment.

Fault A crack in Earth's crust, along which there is movement of one side relative to the other. Faults usually occur in rigid rocks, which tend to break rather than bend.

Fold A bend or buckle in rock caused by intense pressure. Folds usually occur in elastic rocks, which tend to bend rather than break.

Fossil The ancient remains or traces of a once-living thing, usually found preserved in rock.

Geyser A natural fountain of hot water or steam blasted out from a hole in the crust. A geyser erupts when underground water is heated by hot, volcanic rocks.

Glacier A mass of ice produced by the accumulation of snow that moves gradually downhill. It picks up rocky material as it goes, which it later deposits as moraines.

Hadrosaurs "Duck-billed" dinosaurs from the late Cretaceous period. Grazing in herds, they were plant eaters with special grinding teeth.

Igneous rock A type of rock formed from magma that has cooled and hardened.

Lava Magma that has reached Earth's surface through volcanoes or fissures.

Lithosphere Earth's outer layer: its crust and part of the upper mantle.

Magma Hot melted, or molten, rock that is formed mainly in Earth's upper mantle, but also deep in the crust.

Magnetic field The region surrounding a magnet, an object which has two poles, and a force of attraction between them.

Magnetism The invisible force of attraction or repulsion between materials, especially those made of iron.

Magnetosphere The region surrounding Earth in which its magnetic field exerts a force.

Mantle The layer of Earth that lies between the crust and outer core.

Metamorphic rock A rock that has changed due to intense pressure or heat. Metamorphic rocks can form from igneous rocks, sedimentary rocks, or even other metamorphic rocks.

Meteor A mass of rock or metal that has entered Earth's atmosphere, often forming a streak of light as it burns.

Meteorite A meteor that reaches the surface of Earth.

Mid-oceanic ridge A long mountain range under the ocean, where magma rises to Earth's surface.

Mineral A natural chemical substance that is neither plant nor animal. Rocks are made up of minerals. Minerals are the most common solid material found on Earth.

Ocean trench A long, narrow, deep valley in the ocean floor.

Ornithischians The "bird-hipped" dinosaurs, one of two major types of dinosaur (the other is saurischian). Ornithischians had backward-slanting pubic bones—the lower part of the hip bone.

Pterosaurs Flying reptiles that existed from the late Triassic to late Cretaceous periods. Their wings were formed from skin flaps between the fourth finger and lower body.

Saurischians The "lizard-hipped" dinosaurs, one of two major types of dinosaur (the other is ornithischian). Saurischians had forward-jutting pubic bones—the lower part of the hip bone.

Sauropods Long-necked, four-legged, plant-eating dinosaurs. They were the very largest and heaviest land animals of all time.

Seamount An underwater mountain formed by volcanic eruptions.

Sedimentary rock A type of rock that is formed by the pressing together of rock fragments or the remains of living things.

Sediments Eroded rock fragments that are transported by wind, water, or ice and laid down elsewhere.

Silica A compound of silicon and oxygen, silica is found in most of the minerals that make up Earth's crust and mantle.

Subduction The process by which the edge of one crustal plate slips beneath another. The place where this occurs is called a subduction zone.

Tectonic plates The large slabs into which Earth's surface is divided. The plates move relative to one another in a process called plate tectonics, which helps explain the theory of continental drift.

Theropods All the meat-eating saurischian dinosaurs.

Vertebrates Animals that have backbones.

Volcano An opening in Earth's crust through which magma erupts. The name is usually used to describe a cone-shaped mountain with a central vent and a crater at the summit.

Water cycle The process by which water circulates from the land or oceans to the atmosphere and back again.

INDEX

Page numbers in **bold** refer to main entries.